Leaving A-holiness Behind

From Pious Jerk to Not-So-Pious Jerk

By Christian Piatt

Published in the United States by CrowdScribed, LLC
Library of Congress Cataloging-in-Publication

Typeset by CrowdScribed in conjunction with Lightning Source, La Vergne, Tennessee. Printed in the United States by Lightning Source on acid-free paper. Set in Avenir Next Regular

ISBN: 9781945455995
Available in Ebook.

TABLE OF CONTENTS

HELP US CHANGE THE CONVERSATION

If you have this book, you probably agree that some things about Christianity have to change. Big time. We've gotten so far away from what was originally intended that people often struggle to see the connections between what we say and do, and what Jesus said and did. And I haven't just wanted to write this book for five years because we need to be able to laugh (though that's part of it).

We can change the world for the better. For everyone, and not just Christians. And I am just audacious enough to believe that this book can be a part of that change. Now, since you are reading it, so can you. But people have to know about it in order to do anything. For that, I need your help.

Here are some things you can do to have an impact:

- Post reviews on Amazon, Goodreads, BN.com, iBooks, etc: This is quick and easy to do, but it helps a whole lot.
- Share on social media: Take photos of you with the book to share on Facebook, Pinterest, Instagram Tumblr and Twitter. Be sure to tell people why you love it and include a link to where they can get a copy.
- Buy copies for friends and loved ones: It's a great conversation piece and it gives you something to talk and laugh about with them. But you're also helping this independent publishing effort become sustainable.

We don't make much on book sales. We do it because we believe in the work. But we also depend on you, our readers, more than you can imagine. Thank you for what you've already done. You committed to this idea just because you believe in me, my work and the concept. That's amazing. Now I trust we'll keep this going together.

Much love,

Christian

PLEASE ALLOW ME TO INTRODUCE MYSELF

This is a book about assholes, which means it's about pretty much everyone. Not you of course. Just everyone else (don't tell them). More specifically, this book is about asshole Christians, because that's something I know plenty about. But just to make sure we all are on the same page, let's take a moment to bring a few great heroes down to our more familiar asshole level.

Mother Theresa was an amazing woman. She dedicated her life to God, and to serving the poorest of the poor in Calcutta. That's definitely more noble than anything I ever did. Hell, once I was so proud of myself I just had to tell my friend that the food vendor at a soccer game gave me too much change and I gave it back. Yay me!

But Mother Theresa admitted that she struggled to love those she served, sometimes feeling like the only thing allowing her to keep loving them was to serve them. It's also weird to consider that a woman who has been sainted and is considered a holy woman wasn't even sure that she believed in God. Awkward.

Martin Luther King arguably did more to advance civil rights for African-Americans in the Untied States than anyone else of his time. But he also cheated on his wife, and some questioned the size of his ego. Even Gandhi, the image of gentleness and peace, has been accused of spousal abuse, and had some questionable views when it came to women's rights.

The good news is that, if we're all an asshole at one time or another, we all have something in common.

The world has enough self-serious books written by nerds about why religion is great, why it sucks or whatever. The rest of us are just trying to live better lives, understand who we are and what we're meant to do with our lives. Too often religion ends up being yet another demand on our time, another to-do, another item to check off the list just so we don't feel guilty about ignoring it.

But does it offer what we really need? If so, why do so many Christians seem to be such....well, you know. I know, and I'm one of them. So I don't want to read one more article or book trying to telling insiders how to save the Church or telling outsiders why they should go back. I don't care if you go to church or not. That's not the point. This book is meant to do a few things.

First of all, we have to stop being so damn serious. When I was in college there was a small circuit of "Christian comedians" who would make the rounds to schools and churches. They were nice enough folks and meant well, but they all shared one common flaw: they weren't funny. It took me a while to figure out why, because when they weren't performing they could keep a room laughing for hours. But I realized their bits weren't funny because there was this sort of unspoken set of rules they all had to follow:

1. No profanity or any suggestive or provocative material of any kind
2. No slamming the church or Christianity as a whole, and no making fun of Christians
3. Always have an altar call at the end when you try to convert people

But for humor to really work we have to be able to laugh at ourselves, to have our quirks and flaws pointed out and accept that imperfection – and sometimes even being pretty screwed up – doesn't mean we're worthless. Humor also comes from pushing boundaries, from being confronted with the unexpected, so there's so much comedic material that's usually off-limits n church or other Christian circles.

Basically we take "funny" by the throat with a kung fu grip until it promises to behave. Then we let it go and wonder why it makes anxious little puddles of self-consciousness on the stage. Plus, since everything ultimately has to lead one place (saving souls), there's really not much surprise left.

Why do we do this?

The simple answer is, "Because we're assholes." It's true; all of us are. I am. And even if I don't know you I'm going to lay odds you can be a little jerky sometimes too. It's part of human nature. But it doesn't mean we have to default to that. We are capable of more, and we deserve better. At its best, studying and following a way of life inspired by what Jesus did and said should be a way out of this bad habit that's so easy to slip back into. And yet we find some way to take the very thing that should help make it better and use that to make it even worse.

And then we wonder why nobody takes Christianity seriously. In the infinitely wise words of my seven-year-old, Zoe, "Well duh!"

So yeah, we need to be able to laugh, both at ourselves, and especially at the ways we fall short. We screw up, and so what? Instead of admitting it, shaking our heads and screwing up yet again and trying hard to make it right, we try to cover it up with some illusion of self-righteousness, be it from inside religion or outside of it. But jerky behavior is jerky behavior, period.

So let's to leave our a-holiness behind, shall we? And maybe if we get back to some basics - the kind of stuff we know but would rather ignore, the stuff we learned back when we were five, and the sort of stuff Jesus seemed to really mean, like a lot - we'll probably all be a little bit better off.

And hey, if we can have some fun while we're sorting it out, why not? Like I said above, part of the source of healing both for Christians and those hurt by it is found in naming the imperfections and mistakes, laughing at them when we can and then working on getting better at it going forward. My hope for this book is that it will at least help with the first two things, and maybe even offer some new says to think about what it means when we think of the word "Christian."

So relax, have some fun with it, and let's try and get over ourselves. We only get one life as far as we know, and we're in this life together. Let's not waste it being assholes toward each other. Maybe we learn something in the process, and maybe not. But what's the risk in being open to the possibility that, at least maybe, we are here for a little bit more. And maybe if more of us can come to terms with it, this planet we share will be better off for it.

It's worth a try at least. We're worth it.

HOLE-IER THAN THOU

My name is Christian, and I'm an asshole. There was a time when I was pretty sure all Christians were assholes, and based on the God they kept telling me about, I was pretty sure God might be kind of an asshole too.

It seemed to me that Christianity was about getting saved so you wouldn't be a jerk anymore. But the problem was, a lot of the most obnoxious, intolerant, hateful people I knew called themselves Christians. Then I heard a sermon by my friend which started with, "I'm a Christian because I'm an asshole." She didn't try to shrug it off; she embraced it. Not proudly, but fully and honestly. She needed what she found in Jesus every day, all over again because she was an asshole.

Why aren't more Christians like this?

Churches tend to feed peoples' sense of arrogance, superiority and entitlement by telling them they're right and everyone else is wrong. As if their faith was some kind of one-and-done spiritual plastic surgery. We're all screwed up at some basic level; the real problem comes when we think we're above the brokenness. And why bother, when we live in a world that venerates assholes to near sainthood status (see: Donald Trump, Jersey Shore, Charlie Sheen, The Bachelorette... need I go on?)?

I've heard tons of stories of redemption, but most of them end up bothering me more than encouraging me. Generally, it's because all of the bad stuff they talk about in their lives is always referred to in the past tense, and once they're "saved" (still not sure what that means), everything is sunshine and rainbows.

But if this was the case, and if becoming a Christian really cured us once and for all of being assholes, why do so many people in the world see us as judgmental, opportunistic, narrow-minded hypocrites?

Bless Me, Father, for I'm an asshole

I'm not Catholic, but I tend to think that they have something right with the way they start out their confessions. Sure, they always begin with "bless me Father, for I have sinned," but maybe the new, revised version could be:

Bless me, Father, for I'm an asshole.

I'm pretty sure if people of faith would operate first from this perspective, we could avoid an awful lot of the crap done in the name of God and religion. But the problem isn't that we're all assholes; it's that a lot of folks aren't onto the fact that they are. And some of the biggest offenders are Christians.

When I was seventeen years old, I had a Bible thrown at my head and I was invited not to return to my church youth group. Suffice it to say I took them up on that offer.

The problems began when I started thinking for myself. For one, my parents sent me to this private school where we were taught to look at everything with a critical eye, not to take anything at face value, and to arrive at our own conclusions about things based on a thorough analysis of the evidence.

And then I'd go to church and have my youth leader tell me that, contrary to the cases made in my science textbooks, the earth actually was 5,000 years old, and that people used to ride around on dinosaurs like the Lone Ranger or something. He even told me once that scientists were conspiring together to fabricate this so-called fossil record to convince the blind, unthinking masses that the planet was a byproduct of evolution and was much older than the Bible told us it was.

Yes, there literally were two people named Adam and Eve who got tricked by a talking snake. Okay, I'd say, but who did their kids marry? If they were the only ones on the planet, and assuming they had to have sex to keep the species going, doesn't that mean we're all descendants of incest?

Let's just put a pin in that one and move on.

But I didn't want to move on. It didn't make sense, and I wanted answers. I couldn't get over what an asshole God was made out to be in the Bible; smiting people, afflicting them with diseases, setting them up for tests of faith nobody should have to endure and - hello - how about the whole Garden of Eden story? I could see it happening like this:

"Okay kids, here's the deal," says God, "all of this is yours. You don't even have to work for it. But there's just one thing..."

There's always just one thing.

"See that tree in the middle of the garden?"

"Ooh, yeah," says Adam, licking his chops, "that looks awesome."

"Yeah," says God, "it's the best one here. Don't touch it."

"Why not?"

"Because."

"Because why?"

"Well, because if you eat that fruit you'll know everything," says God.

"Sounds like a good thing," says Eve.

"Well, it's not," says God.

"Why not?"

"Add that to the list of things you don't need to know."

"But wait," says Eve, "if we're the only ones here and we can't touch that tree, and if you made all of this, why bother making the tree?"

"Well," says God, "because I need an illustration for the nature of free will, and to point out that, no matter how much you humans ever have, and no matter how good your life is, there will always be something else you'll want."

"Do what?" says Adam.

"Never mind," says God. "Just don't touch it, okay?"

Feels like a setup, if you ask me.

Then there's Noah, the great-grandfather of Biblical do-over stories. He and his family were supposedly the only human beings spared the devastation of the great flood. Obviously he had some serious leverage with the Big Guy, or maybe he just had some incredible carpentry skills, but it turns out Noah was quite the lush. After the family made their way back to dry land, he got his drink on and passed out in his tent with his junk hanging out.

So this is the best God could do? This is the one guy whose family wasn't worth sending to a watery grave on the entire planet?

And while we're on the subject of the ark, there's not enough fuzzy math in the world to explain how two of every single creature fit on this boat built by hand by one guy without power tools.

Well, God is magic, we argue. Maybe God gave Noah superhuman construction powers, or maybe he gave him some kind of holy shrink ray to miniaturize all the critters to pocket size. Maybe he dehydrated them and kept them in little baggies until they got back to land, and then sprinkled them back to their reconstituted selves.

Fine. But if God could do all that, why not just zap the boat into existence in the first place? And if there's not normally enough water on the planet to flood everything, where did all the extra water come from? And where did it go when the flood receded? And did he actually have to trap all of the birds, or did they just fly around and land in the water? What about the fish, whales, protozoa, land-dwelling bacteria...

Well, we'll just have to get back to that.

I'm guessing that the bible college training my youth leaders had received hadn't exactly prepared them for the onslaught of questions I had about pretty much every story we covered. Why would a loving God ask Abraham to kill his own child? Come to think of it, why would God do pretty much the same thing to his own son, setting up Jesus to be the ultimate fall guy for something he didn't do? If Jesus could forgive peoples' sins in the New Testament, why did he have to die for our sins? Was it a problem of volume? And what about the poor schmucks who died before Jesus came along? Or people who never heard about him?

How about my friends from school, half of whom were Jewish? Weren't they worshipping the same God we were? Wasn't Jesus a Jew? Would God seriously throw his Chosen People under the bus because they didn't take some pledge of fidelity to Jesus as their lord and savior? And where in scripture is this oath we all take anyway?

What about my dad? Sure, he's not perfect, and he never goes to church. Our relationship is hardly perfect; 'Awesome Family' magazine isn't exactly panting to feature us on next month's cover, but he loves me. I know it. And I love him.

Sorry kid, but your dad and all those other people are screwed.

So I started doing some thinking on my own about this God they were presenting to me. He made us imperfect, gave us free rein to make our own choices, seems to have set up a world where we're doomed to fail, and then He tosses us into a pit of eternal fire (which He also made) if we don't take some pledge that Christians invented some time after Jesus' death and before I came along.

If that's what this whole Christianity thing is about, and if the rest of my life is supposed to be committed to saving other people from this pit of despair created by the God we're supposed to worship and love, then I'm not sure I want to have anything to do with it.

And that's when my youth minister threw the Bible at me.

I was an asshole, and I knew it in no uncertain terms. Worse than being your average, run-of-the-mill a-hole, I was an apostate. I had put my own salvation in jeopardy, and in asking so many questions, I was dragging others down the slippery slope of eternal darkness with me. I was practically the left hand of the Evil One himself. I was garbage.

I was the ballast, the Achilles' heel in the church's blueprint for salvation. Sure, the signs outside of their buildings told me I was welcome, but I knew better. They didn't want me any more than I wanted them.

So I said so long, and good riddance.

Jesus Loves You, but Everyone Else Thinks You're an Asshole

It wasn't until about a decade later that I came to understand that Jesus actually was pretty fond of folks like me. As I dipped my toe in the waters of the Gospels on my own terms, I found a different kind of Jesus than the one I had known in my childhood.

I didn't find any stories about him condemning gay people to hell. I didn't see anything about him telling people to change or else. The stuff he cared about was a lot of the same stuff I cared about:

Mercy for the poor.

A place at the table for the outcast.

Love for even the least lovable among us.

Hope for a world whose collective love might just be a little bit greater than the sum total of its hurt and assholery.

Sounds like a guy I'd like to know a little more about. Sounds like someone I could even follow for a while, to see where this path leads.

Coming to know what Jesus was about wasn't about becoming perfect, holier than thou, infallible or any of that. It didn't mean I had to adopt the stereotypical lilting, southern drawl, get giant caps on my teeth (I'm more of a gold caps man) and use insane amounts of product in my hair (I'm bald, sorry). I didn't have to wear garish polyester suits or yell at everyone who walked by with a bullhorn. I didn't have to scare them into thinking and acting like me.

I didn't even have to use the King James translation of the Bible. I know, crazy, right???

My friend who preached the "asshole Christian" message

affected me because there was no point in her talk where she drew the invisible line in the room, placed herself on one side and ushered everyone else across it. She didn't have all the answers, and she was still figuring out what it meant to follow Jesus. She screwed it up, all the time, and she readily admitted it.

But that was precisely what kept drawing her to the life and teaching of Jesus. I still don't buy into the idea that becoming a Christian - whatever that means - automatically makes us less of an asshole. And I definitely don't think being a Christian is something we "become" once, and then we're done, as if we've undergone a spiritual oil change.

Could it be that this idea of redemption is less like some stamp we get in life's passport, but more of a lifelong orientation toward something for which we long, but that we'll never entirely reach? Could it be that stories about resurrection and healing in the Bible are less tests of faith to see if we are true believers, and more about a promise that, when we place honest, genuine hope at the center of our lives, things can ultimately be made right? Or at least better?

I'm a heretic, and I've come to terms with that. According to some people, I may not even be a Christian. But I'm a lot less concerned with what they think about me these days. Instead, I take a few steps along the path, curious but a little freaked out about where it's leading. I peel back another layer of my own judgment, anger and asshole-ish-ness as I have the courage, and try to figure out what, if anything, is underneath it all.

Does God make assholes? I'm afraid so. Does God love assholes? Man, I sure hope so.

A QUICK A**HOLE SURVEY

> Feel free to take this yourself, or use it with folks you meet who may or may not be an asshole Christian. Each "YES" response gets a point, and then you can rate your own or others' asshole-osity on the asshole meter at the end.*

1. Do you assume anyone who calls themselves a Christian think and believe like you?
2. Have you ever asked a pastor if they "preach the Bible?"
3. Have you ever driven a gas-powered vehicle to a climate meeting or rally ?
4. Have you ever used a phrase like "Everything happens for a reason," "He/she is in a better place," or "Have you asked Jesus into your heart?"
5. Do you put one of those little Jesus fish on your company sign or business cards? (Half credit if you shop intentionally at places who do.)
6. Have the words "The Bible clearly says..." ever come out of your mouth?
7. Have you ever left a tract instead of a tip for wait staff?
8. Do you believe that pastors who tell you Jesus wants you to be rich are actually preaching the Gospel?
9. Have you ever worn Christian swag to make sure other people know you love Jesus?

10. Do you believe Jesus would have been a republican?

11. Do you believe Jesus would have been a democrat?

12. Do you believe that liking articles you agree with online or forwarding a tweet is an act of social justice?

13. Does your God hate all the same people you do?

14. Have you ever found a way to work one of your own acts of kindness or generosity into a conversation or a social media post as a sort of "humble brag?" (Ex: *"I'm so grateful for the chance to feed the homeless on my day off today !"*)

15. Have you ever used your faith to exclude anyone from full participation and leadership in a faith community? (*Double credit if you've pulled text from the Bible to justify doing so.*)

16. Have you used your faith to deny anyone rights that you already have because they're different than you?

17. Do you feel like Christians have nothing apologize for the things done to others in the name of the Christian faith?

18. Do you talk about your own faith more than you listen?

19. Have you ever made fun of "those Christians?"

20. Do you think the point of evangelism is getting people to come to worship?

21. Do you think that giving to charity or to your church is enough to let you off the hook for the brokenness and suffering in the world?

22. Have you ever told someone that "God helps those who help themselves?"

23. You'd have nothing to say if Jesus asked you "what have you done for the poor?"

24. You want to get more young people into your church so they'll give enough money to save your church.

25. Do you think that your church is what matters most about your faith?

26. Do you think you have to have THE answer to questions any time anyone asks you about your faith?

27. Do you think Jesus was white?

28. Have you ever quoted a Bible verse to someone to prove you're right and they're wrong? (*Double credit if you later realized that verse wasn't actually in the Bible. Triple credit if someone else had to point out to you that the verse wasn't actually in the bible.*)

29. You believe that God's sense of justice is the same as your justice.

30. You think the United states is a Christian nation.

31. Have you ever argued that the world is 6,000 years old?

32. Have you ever judged other people or their actions as "sinful" while not laying out ALL of your own sins for the world to see?

33. Do you think that being pro life is only about abortion?

34. Do you think that answers are more important than questions?

35. Have you ever tried to guilt others for not ascribing to your faith-based eating or shopping choices?

36. Do you believe that the main point of Christianity is avoiding going to hell?

37. Do you believe that God can be both radically loving and still send people to an eternity of conscious torment for something done during their life?

38. Have you ever judged or condemned the immorality of "The Rich," while convinced you're not one of them?

39. Do you believe God actively blesses your already comfortable, privileged life while doing nothing about sex slavery, genocide, child labor and famine?

40. Do you think you're not actually an asshole. (BONUS - worth ten points.)

*The author, publisher, illustrators and all others involved in the creation of this survey are not held liable for any violence done toward your person in conducting this survey with others. We are hereby exempt from all acts of retribution, from flaming poop on your doorstep to permanently reorganized faces. Why? Because we're assholes and bullies scare us.

SCALE/ASSHOLE METER HERE:

0 - 10 POINTS: Ground-level asshole

You'd have to work for folks to recognize you as an asshole Christian on a daily basis.

11 - 20 POINTS: Asshole-in-training

You do some pretty dickish stuff, but you may actually be onto yourself.

21 - 30 POINTS: Executive asshole

Chances are you could make a living at this. When folks talk about Christians being assholes, at least a few people have imagined you.

31 - 40 POINTS: Asshole overload

It's time for an asshole intervention. Like, right now. Stop what you're doing and find some super honest people who don't think or believe like you to tell you how the world really sees you. And until you do, please stop calling yourself a Christian. Better yet, just don't say anything at all.

41 OR MORE POINTS: Asshole Apocalypse

Wow. Just wow, dude.

AN A**HOLE SAYS WHAT?

Growing up, I loved to read books. My favorite author, like many of my peers, was Dr. Seuss. I wore out several copies of "The 500 Hats of Bartholomew Cubbins," Seuss' famous A-B-C book and "The Lorax." But of all of his classics, my favorite by far was "Horton Hears a Who."

I loved that Horton stood up for the little guy (I was not the 7'10" giant I am now in my younger days). He was so careful and attentive, even though he was so much bigger and stronger than most of the other animals in the jungle. But what really made me love Horton was his famous saying:

"I meant what I said, and I said what I meant. An Elephant's faithful, one-hundred percent."

It's a highly underrated virtue, saying what we mean and meaning what we say. We live in a data-saturated world where we spend more time filtering through the mire of information, coming toward us in a constant flood, than we used to exert seeking out the stuff we actually wanted. The voice that gets heard these days often is the loudest or most shocking, rattling the cages of the otherwise cynical public until someone takes notice. It's easy to make incremental compromises in what words we chose until suddenly, the things we say every day seem to have lost any real meaning.

We Christians have a remarkable talent for sticking our feet in our mouths. We're known for always having something to say, whether it's welcome or not. We want to share a little bit with you about our faith, tell you why you should believe the same way we do, why you should come to our church, and we really love a chance to drop some divine wisdom on others to help give their life meaning.

But too often, we become the noisy gongs and clanging cymbals we're warned about in I Corinthians. Paul's point in that passage is that it doesn't matter how nice the words we say happen to be, because if they're not said with the full backing of divinely inspired love, they don't really mean much of anything.

What's worse, we end up acting like jerks.

The funny thing about cliches is they're not technically lies. Unless you use one you know isn't true, usually it's a sin of negligence. We often feel compelled to say something, and the first thing that pops out (because of training, cultural conditioning or simple thoughtlessness) is a cliché.

It's kind of like the fart that sneaks out when you're trying to sneeze. Except rather than simply embarrassing yourself, you may actually be doing lasting harm to others.

If you search the words most commonly associated with "Christian," you'll find the list isn't pretty. Part of this can be attributed to a handful of phrases that, if stricken from your vocabulary, might make you much more tolerable. Yes, these phrases may mean something to some people, but trust me, not everyone outside of Christianity shares a love for them. And more than a few within the Christian community are weary of them too.

I've divided the clichés into eight groups:

1. Best Intentions
2. Loaded Questions
3. Fear and Trembling
4. Backhanded Judgment
5. I'm Saved but You Suck
6. Conversation Killers, and
7. Awkward...

Some may be all too familiar. You may even use some of them. But before tossing the book across the room, try to sit with these a while and consider how they might sound to someone who doesn't think, feel or believe the way you do. Also, some of these are not exclusively Christian.

Though that doesn't make using them any better.

I hope you'll be entertained by this list rather than convicted, implicated, or infuriated. Take a chance to have a laugh, even if it's at your own expense, or share them with a friend or loved one to see if they agree. And let me know if I left any out or if some should stay in the Christian vocabulary. Personally, I won't be offended if you take my advice to avoid these or not, as long as you take Horton's sage advice:

"Mean what you say, and say what you mean."

1. BEST INTENTIONS

"Everything happens for a reason."

I've heard this said more times than I care to count. I'm not sure where it came from either, but it's definitely not in the Bible. The closest thing I can come up with is "To everything, there is a season," but that's not exactly the same.

But faith, by definition, is not reasonable. If it could be empirically verified with facts or by using the scientific method, it wouldn't be faith. It would be a theory. Also, consider how such a pithy phrase sounds to someone after something really horrible happened. Do we really think God had a reason to allow that to happen? Even if it's true, which is debatable, I don't even want to hear that if I only lost my car keys. I don't want a reason; I want my keys.

And what I really want is someone who understands what it's like to lose something important to me. Someone who will be quiet, listen, and empathize with me. But don't dismiss grief, tragedy or even struggle with such a meaningless phrase.

"God needed another angel in heaven, so He called them home."

Honestly, saying anything when someone is grieving can be well-meaning but insensitive. This one assumes a lot about the person's beliefs, and also ignores the grief they're going through. Just don't.

With grief, the trouble comes when we want to skirt the real issue. The person who died is, well, dead. What bothers the grieving most is when we act as though they need protecting from that fact. The death happened. It was not just uncomfortable. And what the grieving need is someone who can focus on the needs of the living right in front of them, who won't try to cover over things with divine providence, and face the music. God doesn't have empty spaces on in some holy angel choir that need filling. People die, and it sucks.

"The Lord never gives someone more than they can handle." Bullsh**. Sorry, I have to call B.S. on this one. It's far too common and it deserves to be taken out back and shot. God never gives anyone more than they can handle? I see. Except for people in car accidents who end up with profound mental illness. Or people in war-torn countries who are tortured to death. Or maybe just the millions of people who die every day.

Plenty of folks end up with more than they can handle, and although the crisis at hand may not be as grave as death, it often is bad, and it tends to minimize the struggle the person is going through. They *feel* like they can't handle all they're "given," so what does that say about them? Without meaning to, we're implying they're weak, unable to bear their own burden that God assigned to them.

This also implies that, if really horrible things are happening to them, God gave it to them. So is this a test? Are they being punished? Is God just arbitrarily cruel? I'm pretty sure I wouldn't be a big fan of that God. Now, I do believe that, in hindsight there are plenty of things we didn't think we could handle. And sometimes, looking back, we realize that the thing we thought was so incredibly awful wasn't as bad as we thought. Maybe it even led to something pretty good. At least maybe it helped toughen us up or glean some wisdom from the experience.

But if you're like me, if life has just given me a swift kick in the goodie bag, the last thing I want to hear is that God did it to me, and that I can handle it. Just get me some ice.

"When God closes a door, He opens a window."

Like the cliché above, this implies that when something unexpected (and usually bad) happens to us, God did it to us. I know it may be offered with the best of intentions, but it's not helpful in most cases.

What about someone who feels like the door has closed on them, and there is no other hope in sight? What if their hand was in the door? Or what if it was a door they hoped to escape their horrible life out of and they felt God assured them there was freedom on the other side?

Oh, but fear not; there's still a great window you can try to climb out of!

Folks who are struggling will benefit more from a compassionate ear, a loving heart and a simple "What can I do to help?" much more than some phrase that may or may not have any basis in reality.

"If you just have enough faith, it will happen for you."

Talk about setting God up! I've often thought it must take the testicular fortitude of an MMA fighter to speak with authority about what God will or will not do in others' lives. Sure, if we have a story of personal experience to share, it might make sense to ask for permission to share it. But be aware that someone in the midst of a struggle might not be particularly interested in hearing said story, even if it's done with the intention of offering hope.

Making such promises is above our spiritual pay grade. As my dad used to say, don't write checks your butt can't cash.

Also, it implies that the quality of life we enjoy (or are subjected to) has a direct correlation with our faithfulness. If I lost my job last month, it must have been because I skipped church that one time. If I found a $100 bill on the ground, must be because of that super-extra awesome prayer over the spam casserole at dinner! Some people do believe this is how the universe works, but it also seems to paint a picture of a rather superficial, transactional God.

It's "divine physics" based on magical thinking. Kind of like what's suggested by "everything happens for a reason," it says we must deserve what comes to us. Which leads to Pat Robertson saying levees breaking and devastating New Orleans are because of America's policy on abortion. Which leads to that old line about an angel dying every time you masturbate.

God, I sure hope that one's a myth

"That's just another jewel in your crown."

This may not make a lot of sense to some non-Christians, but I've heard it my entire life. Basically, it suggests that doing good or enduring something builds up the rewards you will receive in heaven. This is a gross distortion of what Jesus taught. He didn't teach us to have selfish motives either now or after we die; he taught us to get over ourselves entirely.

If we look at biblical stories like the prodigal son or the vineyard laborers, we're all treated to God's love equally in the sweet by-and-by. In short, we should aim to stop doing things for some expected reward, whether in this life or the next. Do it because it's the right thing to do.

Plus, who really wants to go around in a crown? Seriously!

"They're in a better place."

This may or may not be true. Again, we have no real way of knowing. We may believe it, or we may hope. We have faith that it's true, but at best it's unhelpful, and at worst, it's dismissive and arrogant. It minimizes the grief of the people they left behind.

One thing Jesus was best at was noticing needs right in front of him and addressing them as they came up. One of his greatest gifts was how completely present he was to whoever he was with. He connected deeply with them, which is really, really hard. Definitely harder than saying something like "she's in a better place," and getting back to our *Seinfeld* reruns before any feelings ooze out all over the place.

"God is in control" or "God is always good."

These raise the very serious problem of *theodicy*. And most Christians I've met who say these things are not prepared to address it. Basically, believing in an all-knowing, all-loving and all-powerful God doesn't gel with the existence of evil and suffering in the world. If God is both all-powerful and all-loving, then why do innocent people die? Or actually, why in the hell do the Mavericks lose? That's obviously not reconcilable.

If we have free will (which most Christians think we do), that's a necessary forfeit of some control by God. So probably good to be careful before presuming to know how big a role God plays in daily life. Telling someone who was abused, tortured, neglected, etc. that God was good or in control during that experience—whether it's true or not—is not likely to motivate them to appreciate the concept of God's love, grace and mercy.

When you attempt to engage in theodicy and defend God's goodness in the face of evil, you heap a whole mess of guilt onto that person's grief. And that is, not to contradict Martha Stewart, *not* a good thing.

2. LOADED QUESTIONS

"Have you asked Jesus into your heart?"

I do think that taking the example and teaching of Jesus to heart is a life-giving and important step in healing or "salvation" in many forms. But as many times as I've heard this question, I still don't really know what it means. Why my heart? Why not my liver or kidneys? It makes Christianity sound like a purely emotional experience rather than a lifelong practice that can never entirely be realized. But yeah, asking someone if they're engaged in a lifelong discipline to orient their lives toward Christ-like compassion, love and mercy doesn't exactly have the same ring to it.

Not that that's not an awesome idea. It just makes a bad question. Ultimately I like a well-known quote from an unknown source about this subject: "Preach the Gospel at all times and when necessary use words."

If you've just met someone, doesn't this seem–I don't know–pretty intimate? It makes me want to respond with, "I'll tell you if you tell me what kind of underwear you have on." It's kind of a relational violation. And if it's a person you know well, you probably don't need to ask. You'll be able to tell how seriously they take the whole "following Jesus" thing.

On the other hand, if you're just asking to make sure they've said the right set of words to go to heaven, like the Secret

Salvation Handshake, that's not helping anyone. Better to do everyone a favor and just listen for a while instead of talking.

"Have you accepted Jesus as your personal Lord and Savior?"

Jesus refers to himself in third person a lot, like Lebron James. But he never calls himself "Lord and Savior." Though we have King James English to thank for the lord part, the phrase is actually from the Nicene Creed, which was created by the Nicene Council (makes sense, right?) after Constantine, Rome's emperor at the time, declared Christianity to be the only legal religion in the Roman Empire.

People who didn't confess Jesus as "Lord and Savior" (as opposed to confessing the deified emperor as "lord and savior," which was a big change) and abandon all other gods and religions could be jailed, exiled or killed. So yeah, historically it's been a little bit of a loaded phrase.

Plus, the whole idea of a lord is so antiquated, it has no relevance to our lives today. I've never met any lords, though I do recall Sean Connery getting knighted. But anyway, the idea of a lord is someone who rules over you in a kind of dictatorial way. And even if the point was that Jesus was a different kind of lord, in my reading of scripture, this isn't what He was about. He was a servant of the people.

Plus it now evokes images of Lord Vader or Lord Voldemort, and we all know those dudes were bad news.

"Are you saved?"

The concept of salvation is a really complicated one, to be sure. And it probably shouldn't be something that could be encapsulated and really understood in a ten-word question. This is pretty damn hard to respond to with a simple yes or no. The root word that "salvation" comes from actually means "healing." And in so much as we're always in varying stages of both healing and brokenness, I guess the answer should always be "yes and no."

Of course, people who ask it just want to know if you have fire insurance. Regardless of whether you believe in a literal hell, this question suggests a power/privilege imbalance (i.e., "I'm saved, but I'm guessing you're not based on some assumptions I'm making about you"), and it leaps over any personal investment or relationship and straight into the deep waters of personal faith.

Again, kinda like the underwear question. *STRANGER DANGER!*

If you take the time to hear someone's story—or better yet, walk alongside them in life—you'll likely learn plenty about what they think and believe in the process. And who knows? You might actually learn something too, rather than just telling others what they should believe.

"Are you Catholic or Christian?"

This one I've heard most often in places where there are more Catholics than any other religion or denomination. Actually, I guess I should specify that I mean places in the United States, because I went to Rome, and no one ever asked me if I was Catholic or Christian.

The question suggests, first of all, that Catholics aren't Christian. Second, it draws firm lines between Catholics and Protestants that (thankfully) have become increasingly blurry in recent years with things like *Taize*-style worship and other "ancient-future" practices.

Yes, I do value much about the Protestant Reformation, placing power of scriptural interpretation in the hands of the faithful rather than the priesthood. But we also lost much that was valuable in our faith, like an emphasis on the Divine Feminine, rituals focusing on spiritual practices, a sense of mysticism rather than certainty, and even the amazing icons and artwork that can be so inspiring, without telling us what to think or believe.

Also, just to clarify, the word "Catholic" means "Universal Church." So technically all Christians are still Catholic. So if you ever get asked that question, you can comfortably just say "yes." Unless you're in Italy; then say "*si*," and ask them to join you for some pasta.

3. FEAR AND TREMBLING

"Jesus died for your sins."

I know this is an all-time Christian favorite. But even if you buy into the concept of substitutionary atonement and that God set Jesus up as a sacrifice to pay for sin, this is a tricky way to introduce the faith to someone. It's kind of like being on a first date and telling her she has hidden emotional problems.

They didn't ask Jesus to die for them, and if they're not weighed down by shame and guilt, they have no concept of how Jesus dying for their sins could be "good news." The whole idea of being dirty and evil and needing Jesus' blood to stand in for ours has given plenty of people genuine emotional problems, not to mention childhood nightmares. It's just the wrong place to start a deeper conversation about what Christianity is about because it tends to make God seem like a big meanie for requiring payment.

So maybe instead of focusing on people's sin, we can focus more on Jesus' Greatest Commandment and Paul's most important human virtue: to learn love. And maybe that means it's got to be received directly from a God who holds no scorecard over our heads, and then instead of using words, we could share it with others with our hands and feet and our time and resources.

"If you died today, do you know where you'd spend the rest of eternity?"

No, I don't, and neither does anyone else. This is a presumptuous question this that implies the questioner has some insider knowledge that the rest of us don't. And seriously, if our faith is entirely founded upon the notion of eternal fire insurance, we're not sharing testimony; we're peddling propaganda.

I can't even be sure where I'm going to sleep tonight because my house could burn down. Nothing is certain. That's not what faith is about. Suffice it to say my certainty about all things future is cloudy at best and life requires a sense of adventure in the midst of all the unknown, i.e. faith. There's no knowing what heaven is like or what's yet to happen.

But whatever heaven is like, I'm still hoping my future involves hover-boards, clothes made out of bacon and time-traveling Deloreans.

"We're living in the end times."

This is one of my favorites. Really? Didn't Jesus say this 2000 years ago? "Truly I tell you, some who are standing here will not taste death before they see the Son of Man coming in his kingdom." (Matt. 16:28) We Christians love to take things literally. We love to believe Jesus actually said exactly the words the Bible writers used many decades after it all happened. Sure, look for signs of the end of the world; explore your apocalyptic fetish. But at least consider that it's possible the world might not end soon, and this statement makes it sound like you can't wait to say "I told you so" to all the nonbelievers.

And this simply won't make anyone say, "Wow. I was not aware of that. Sign me up!"

4. BACKHANDED JUDGMENT

"Love the sinner, hate the sin."

This is a really weird way to try and tell someone you love them. It also ignores Jesus' command not to focus on the shortcomings of our neighbors while we each have a laundry list of screw-ups of our own. Bottom line: we all mess up. But calling someone else a sinner is a jerky move.

Also, the "hate the sin" bit sounds like we're saying, "I hate what you do," "I hate who you are" or "I hate what you stand for," which sort of neutralizes the whole "I love you" implied in the first part.

Just love. When we get that one completely mastered, then we'll talk about judging and stuff.

"The poor dear," or "Bless your heart."

These usually follow one of two less-than-kind statements. Either it's after some kind of thinly veiled insult or after a juicy bit of gossip about the person whose heart you want to be "blessed": "Did you hear Nancy's husband got caught sleeping with his secretary? Bless her heart," or, "He's not exactly the sharpest tool in the shed, bless his heart."

Anyone from the south knows what I'm talking about.

People who say such things must be working toward an honorary masters in how to lose friends and alienate people, while also sounding like a craven gossip. Bless their hearts.

"They are a good, strong, God-fearing Christian."

I actually heard this when buying our house. The sellers were glad to be selling their home to "strong Christians." I'm not sure what they based this on since they knew almost nothing about us, but I expect it had to do with the fact that we both work in ministry.

That, or they noticed my buns of steel.

The whole thing leans on so many assumptions and personal biases, while also casting a plenary judgment on those so-called "bad" or "weak" Christians. It contributes to the country club mentality of Christianity that there are some people doing it

right and many doing it wrong. And, of co
the judgment is always on the right side.

The phrase "God-fearing" is a real turn-o
Christians and non-Christians alike. Though some unde
God as a thing to be feared, a lot of folks do not. And if yo
happen to be using the word "fear" as a synonym for "respect," consider the likelihood that your audience probably hears "fear" as "fear." If you mean "respect," say "respect."

"I'm praying for you."

I had a guy say this to me last week who was not a fan of my work. And although I'm sure sometimes people mean well when they say this, often it's basically the religious equivalent of the middle finger ("I don't like you and wish you would change, so I'm going to pray for you to become more like me").

People may say it with truly benevolent intent, but it's still a very personal thing. Instead, consider asking someone if they would like you to pray for them, and ask what they would like you to pray for instead of assuming you know exactly what they need.

"There, but for the grace of God, go I."

I've been guilty of this one more times than I'd like to admit. But it suggests that the person we're referring to is not the recipient

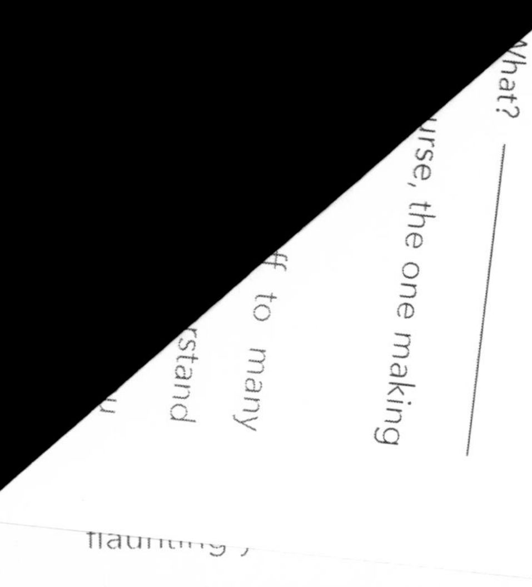

least as I understand it) God's

ıt like party favors. Everyone is a

have no idea how much or how

ıg ourselves.

and even recognizing we share

ıing. But believing this one is like

flaunting ticket even though you know you didn't deserve a penny.

"God helps those who help themselves."

Let's be clear: THIS IS NOT SCRIPTURE. People treat it like it is, but it's not. Benjamin Franklin penned this in the Farmers' Almanac in 1757.

We should be very, very careful when quoting something we think is in the Bible, not to mention what we think the Bible means. And we ought to be careful about how and why we quote it to (and never at) people. People don't need more reasons to resent or resist scripture; let's not add things that aren't even in there.

5. I'M SAVED, BUT YOU SUCK

"Christianity is the only way to God/Heaven."

Folks believe this with their whole heart and they have the

scriptures at the ready to support it. But those we're speaking with think differently, or haven't put much thought into it, so this phrase can feel like an ultimatum. Or a threat.

Yes, there are texts to support a theology of exclusive salvation. But there are several that support universal salvation (John 1:9 - "The true light, which enlightens everyone, was coming into the world.").

Theologically speaking, it opens up a whole bunch of questions about the fate of all those who lived before Christ, who never hear about him, and so on. Salvation (however we come to understand what that means) may ultimately only be made available to humanity by way of Jesus, or at least the unconditional love and grace he embodies. But we also need to stay open to the possibility that God's grace is bigger than our own understanding of it.

"God will do anything to get your attention," or "God's obviously saying something to you."

Here's a tip: if you want to help people: don't speak for God. The better approach might be to look for the good that might come of this event or situation and the wisdom to be found in the experience. Be quiet, be present and be compassionate as you seek to show love.

Let God speak for God. Unless you're trying to show how God might use presumptuous, insensitive commentary to tell someone it's time to get a new friend.

"I don't do that; I'm a Christian."

It's great that we choose to live differently because of our faith. Faith should inform much of our daily life. But making public announcements about it reeks of pride and casts judgment on those who think or act differently than we do. We're exalting ourselves, which I'm pretty sure is something Christians aren't supposed to do.

I know we can find a biblical basis for "boasting in Christ," but if what we're doing makes us look like self-righteous tools, chances are we're not doing it right.

"I don't put God in a box."

First off, this implies others do put God in a box, and that our superior perspective doesn't. Problem is, anyone who says this is putting God in a box: the box of My Superior Theology. All believers put God in a box. Yes, my box may be different than others' boxes, but unless we share the mind of God, our understanding of God is some conscripted, dimly illuminated view of what He actually is. That, my friends, is a box.

Even if your box is really, really big and bedazzled so much it blinds the neighbors, it's still a freakin' box.

"That (sin) is an abomination in the eyes of God."

This phrase is a favorite with the anti-homosexuality crowd. Seldom do these folks care that divorce and remarriage is also a so-called abomination.

Oh, also eating shellfish.

And touching a pig's skin on the Sabbath (take that, Peyton Manning!)

And wearing blended fibers for clothes (regardless of the fact that 100% cotton shrinks and pure linen is an enormous pain in the ass to iron)

There are actually several words translated in English Bibles as 'abomination,' many of which don't imply the sort of exceptionalism the word implies today. And while we're on the subject of what God "hates," let's consider this from Proverbs:

> *These six things doth the LORD hate: yea, seven are an abomination unto him: A proud look, a lying tongue, and hands that shed innocent blood, a heart that deviseth wicked imaginations, feet that be swift in running to mischief, A false witness that speaketh lies, and he that soweth discord among brethren.*

I'll go out on a limb and propose that telling someone who they aren't allowed to be or who they aren't allowed to like is an abomination to God. At the very least, it's sowing discord among your brothers and sisters. And that, according to the text above, is also an abomination.

Talk about irony!

"It was Adam and Eve, not Adam and Steve."

Do I even need to mention this one? This is a little "joke" some Christians *love* to use. But here's the thing: the Bible is full of divinely-sanctioned incest, polygamy and men sleeping with their slaves. In fact, there's practically a how-to manual in scripture about how to treat your slave.

This phrase just demonstrates the selective moral blindness many of us Christians have which should seriously cause us pause about our credibility on matters of gender identification and sexuality. Also, I'm pretty sure if we ever winnow ourselves down to two human beings left, the deed will get done, regardless of orientation.

6. CONVERSATION KILLERS

"The Bible clearly says..."

Hmm. Two points on this one. First, unless you're a biblical scholar who knows the historical and cultural contexts of the scriptures and can read them in their original languages, the Bible isn't "perfectly clear" about much of anything. Yes, we can pick and choose verses that say one thing or another, but by whom was it originally said, and to whom? Cherry-picking scripture to make a point is called proof-texting, and it's a theological no-no.

Second, the Bible can be used to make nearly any point we care to (anyone want to justify slavery?), so let's not use it as a billy club against each other.

"America was founded as a Christian nation."

Really? It's common knowledge that the United States was founded on the principle of religious liberty, but that doesn't mean just the liberty to be a Christian. And many of the founding fathers explicitly were not Christian, at least not in the way many of us might think.

Several were deists, and leaders like Thomas Jefferson and Benjamin Franklin were considered "non-clerical" Christians, meaning they didn't ascribe to the dogmas and authority of the Church. In fact, Jefferson revised the Gospels to align more with his own beliefs, removing all references to the supernatural or miraculous. Not exactly the kind of thing encouraged in most Sunday schools today!

It's more accurate to say that America was founded as a nation of religious liberty. This includes liberty to be Jewish, Muslim, pagan or even atheist. As the familiar trope goes, freedom only for some is actually freedom for none. Freedom to be just like me and nothing else is just authoritarianism.

"The Bible says it; I believe it; that settles it."

If ever there was a top-shelf conversation killer, this is it. We're not inviting any opinion, response, rational thought or discussion of any kind. We're simply making a claim and telling others to shut up.

I've yet to meet someone who takes *every word* of the Bible literally. Everyone qualifies something in it, like the parts about keeping kosher, stoning adulterers, or tossing our rebellious virgin daughters to the hands of an angry mob. Not exactly step one in good neighbor behavior.

Better to say something along the lines of, "I take the Bible seriously," or "I use the Bible to inform my daily behavior." Even better, maybe don't say it at all. If we're really living it out, it should be more than obvious.

"Jesus was a Democrat/Republican."

Seems to me that, when pressed, Jesus was happy to keep church and state separate. Remember the whole thing about giving to

Caesar what is Caesar's, and giving to God what is God's? And if we choose to, we can pick and choose anecdotes to support Jesus being a liberal (care for the poor, anti-death penalty) or a conservative (challenge government authority, practice sexual purity).

Jesus was Jesus, and if it was as simple as pegging him to one of two seriously flawed contemporary forms of government, I can promise you, there would not be a single Christian left. Okay, maybe one guy in Wichita.

7. AWKWARD...

"Will all our visitors please stand?"

This is a great strategy if your goal is to make all newcomers so uncomfortable that a little pee comes out. Or maybe that's just me...

If someone finally is brave enough to walk through the doors of our churches, the last thing they want is to be singled out. They probably don't know the songs we're singing (hell, I still don't recognize half of them) or the prayers or responsive readings we're doing. Depending on the translation of the Bible we use, the scripture may not make much sense, and they probably have no idea where the bathroom is (see: "little bit of pee coming out" above). Why add to the discomfort by making them stand so everyone can stare at them?

Also, calling someone a visitor already implies they are simply passing through, that they're not a part of things. Instead of "visitor" or "guest," try something less loaded like "friend." Better yet, walk up to them, introduce yourself and learn their name. And maybe, if they're comfortable, introduce them to a few folks, one at a time.

But whatever you do, don't be like the couple who came up to me when I was visiting their church and tell them they're in your seat. Wow, did their jaws drop when I got up to guest-preach. I sort of hoped a little pee came out!

"Can I share a little bit about my faith with you?"

Oh. My. God. No. This reminds me of a bit Steve Martin used to do about being grossed out by smokers. He said his go-to response when someone asked if he minded if they smoked was, "Why, no! Mind if I fart?"

Christians claim something—or at least we're meant to be in intentional pursuit of—something everyone else needs, even if they don't identify it themselves. The problem is that we get so caught up in the excitement of sharing what we think someone needs—and therefore what they must not have—that too often we put it all out there before even taking the time to get to know someone as a person, Christian or not. Sadly, this can make us a bit off-putting, presumptuous or pretentious. We should ask someone about their story, but maybe not the second we meet them. Christian evangelism often is the equivalent of a randy young teenager trying to get in good with his new girlfriend. And we know how desperate and sad horny teenagers are (at least boys). Don't be that guy. Nobody likes that guy.

Christians do (or should anyway) have a light, an experiential understanding of love the whole world needs and craves. But many "Christians" don't or haven't had it recently, or have forgotten their experience of the light. So they're trying to muster it up and use hackneyed phrases or make themselves good Christians in hopes of rejuvenating that old faith.

There are worse things we could be doing than trying to share something wonderful with someone, honestly. The trouble is, the kind using this phrase are going about sharing in a very old world, very unsophisticated and ineffective way. And worse, they're trying to prop up their faith by sharing their story with a stranger and maybe seeking a chance for validation or a gold star for their actions. And that's bullsh**.

When our personal agenda is more important than the humanity of the person we're talking to, most people can sense the opportunism from a mile away. Plus we need to stay open to the possibility that such light comes in forms, and with names, we may not personally recognize. Just because it doesn't look like ours doesn't mean it's not light.

"You should come to church with me on Sunday."

It's not that we should never invite people to church, but too much of the time, it's the first thing we do when we encounter someone new. My wife, Amy, and I started a new church eleven years ago, founded on the principle of "earning the right to invite."

We need to invest in people first. Listen to their stories. Learn their passions, their longings, and share the same about ourselves. Then, after we've actually invested in each other, we might try suggesting something not related to church to help us connect on a spiritual level. If the person really gets to know us and wants to know more about why we live our lives the way we do, they'll make a point to find out. And so far, it seems to work better than the agenda-driven sales pitch.

CLICHES AGAINST HUMANITY, THE GAME

Ever played "Cards Against Humanity?" This is our version.

Copy the cliches below and cut them up into individual cards (or cut them straight out of the book if you wanna), shuffle them and turn them over. Deal them out to everyone in the group and you can look at them but keep them secret.

Have the leader read one of the questions or scenarios listed below and let each group member pick a cliche to respond with. Let the group vote on which one is the "best," and that person gets a point.

Of course, this is just a starting place. You can also create your own questions, scenarios and cliches to keep the game going.

QUESTIONS

1. Is God male or female? If so, does God have genitals? Why?

2. My Christian friend got passed up for a big promotion at work, and they gave it to an atheist. What's up with that?

3. My goldfish died, but before he did, I tried to get him to accept Jesus into his heart. Do you think he'll be in heaven?

4. I've had really crappy luck lately. Why is God doing this to me?

5. In one part of the Bible, it says "An eye for an eye, and a tooth for a tooth," but then Jesus said to turn the other cheek. Which one is right?

6. My friend told me that prayer will get me what I want if I do it enough. What do you think?

7. Why does most Christian music suck so much?

8. How come worship is so boring?

9. If Jews are God's chosen people, do they get to go to heaven, even if they don't accept Jesus into their hearts?

10. Why would God create something as terrible and scary as hell if God is supposed to be so loving?

11. I lost my wallet. Will God help me find it if I pray?

12. Why are so many churches shrinking and closing down these days?

13. How many times can I touch my naughty parts and still go to heaven?

14. Aren't Jesus and Buddha more alike than they are different?

15. If you're a Christian, how come you watch R-rated movies and drink beer?

16. Why didn't God just create us with all the knowledge we needed rather than having the Bible written?

17. What happens to people who have never heard of Jesus? What about little kids or babies?

18. When is the world going to end?

19. There are so many different denominations within Christianity. Which one is the right one?

20. The Bible is so confusing and boring. Do I really have to read the whole thing?

Everything happens for a reason	God needed another angel in heaven, so He called him/her home	The Lord never gives someone more than they can handle
When God closes a door, He opens a window	If you just have enough faith it will happen for you	That's another jewel in your crown
You should come to church with me on Sunday	They are in a better place	God is in control
Have you asked Jesus into your heart?	Do you accept Jesus as your personal Lord and Savior?	Are you saved?
Are you Catholic or Christian?	Jesus died for your sins	If you died today, do you know where you'd spend eternity?
We're living in the end times	Love the sinner, hate the sin	Bless your heart

Cut along the dotted lines

They're a good, strong, God-fearing Christian	I'm praying for you	There, but for the grace of God, go I
God helps those who help themselves	Christianity is the only way to God/ Heaven	God will use anything to get your attention
God is obviously saying something to you	I don't do that; I'm a Christian	I don't put God in a box
That is an abomination in the eyes of God	It was Adam and Eve, not Adam and Steve	The Bible clearly says you're wrong
America was founded as a Christian nation	The Bible says it; I believe it; that settles it	Jesus was a Democrat
Jesus was a Republican	Will all our visitors please stand?	Can I share a little bit about my faith with you?

Cut along the dotted lines

JESUS, MY SUPER-AWESOME BOYFRIEND

Most Christians don't watch *Southpark*. Or if they do, they never admit it. It's kind of like the joke about how to keep a Baptist from drinking all your beer: just invite another Baptist. Sometimes we're not as pious as we come across, but I take the pressure off myself by admitting up front that I don't fit–and haven't for most of my life–into the stereotypical mold of what a "good Christian" is. And that includes *Southpark*.

They had a brilliant episode a while back where Cartman got the other boys together to try and form a boy band. I think they were called something totally subtle and not-at-all sexual like 'Finger Bang." Anyway they were a failure, mostly because they sucked. They couldn't even pull off a gig at the local mall. So it looked like their prospects for fame and fortune were dim.

Then Cartman listened to some contemporary Christian music and realized they weren't really any better. In fact, the songs were pretty much the same as the boy band songs, except instead of saying "baby, baby," they said, "Jesus, Jesus." So with a few righteous lyric tweaks (and a necessary name change) they hit the contemporary Christian music circuit and were a huge hit.

Southpark isn't funny because of their incredible animation. Trey Parker and Matt Stone aren't brilliant cartoonists. And it's not because they push the envelope of propriety (some might say destroy it). Anyone can tell poop jokes: even my six-year-old. It's great because the writing names things that most of us know but don't admit, and in a way that helps us laugh at the truth, and maybe even at ourselves a little. Unfortunately, too many Christians are too self-serious to enjoy even a gentle poke at their expense.

But Trey and Matt are right; most Christian music, especially the contemporary stuff, sucks. But why? There are so many talented musicians in churches, and there are lots of great and well-known artists singing out there who also happen to be Christian. So what's the deal with becoming a "Christian musician" that seems to make it all go bad? And come to think of it, what the hell does it mean to be a Christian musician? Is there an official test or something? A sort of Christian illuminati who determines your faith-iness? Some kind of mystical algorithm kept under gilded lock and key in the bowels of some televangelist chapel somewhere that can tell if your songs are Christian enough?

Actually, in a manner of speaking, yeah. There is.

Scary - Bloody - Awesome

I grew up at my mom's feet, watching them rock back and forth as she worked the pedals on her upright piano. Most of my years in grade school, she volunteered as the piano player for the Baptist church we attended, so I got to know all the standard hymns really well. I loved the melodies, and I loved to sit with my head against the wood of the piano, feeling the vibrations murmur through my entire body.

As I got a little older, I started humming harmonies along with her playing, picking out parts above and below her lead. It was like an easy dance that flowed between us, that is until she would play softer to try to hear me singing.

"Why did you stop?" she asked, resting her hands in her lap.

"Because," I said, flipping my shoelace from side to side, "I don't want you to hear me. It's embarrassing."

"If you have a gift," she said, "God says you should share it with others." I shook my head as my cheeks flushed.

"Can you just keep playing?"

As I got into my pre-teen years, I started paying closer attention to the words of a lot of the songs. So many of them were about *death*. Some of my favorites like "I'll Fly Away" and "when the Roll is Called Up Yonder" were all about heading off to a better place when we died. Did old people really spend this much time dwelling on such depressing stuff?

And then there were the ones about Jesus' death. Those were even more graphic. But there was one that stood out from all the rest, called, "There's a Fountain Filled With Blood." That one gave me nightmares for years:

> *There is a fountain filled with blood drawn from*
> *Emmanuel's veins;*
> *And sinners plunged beneath that flood lose all their*
> *guilty stains.*
> *Lose all their guilty stains, lose all their guilty stains;*
> *And sinners plunged beneath that flood lose all their*
> *guilty stains.*

Umm, gross. Not only gross, but pretty terrifying, actually. It brings to mind some Freddy Kruger kind of scene from one of the old *Nightmare on Elm Street* movies, where one poor victim produces several hundred buckets of gore and fluid.

Nasty, right? So why is it considered normal to sing about

it in church? Do you really need to plunge me, head and all, into a pool of blood to be cleansed of my sin? Thanks but no thanks. I think I'll take my chances with the sin.

Then the eighties introduced a new kind of music that was birthed from the spiritual folk songs of the sixties and seventies. Drums and keyboards replaced the dusty old organ-and-choir hymns, and the songs actually made you feel pretty good. They were all about love, praise and good stuff. Nothing like the horror scenes depicted by the old hymnbook.

Instead of being different from "regular" music, this contemporary stuff actually reflected the modern culture around us. One of these songs could just as easily pop up on MTV in between Duran Duran and Eddie Grant as it would before the Sunday sermon. I mean, except for the fact that the music was pretty cheesy and every other word was "Jesus," but it was different, at least.

But my love affair with the likes of Petra and Carmen was short-lived. I was well into my teen years by then, and I had questions. A lot of them. And the folks singing these songs–along with the thousands of people in the stadiums singing along with them, waving their hands in ecstasy–seemed to have it all figured out. They loved Jesus. Like, all the time. It was like they had some great invisible friend, following them around, telling them all the right things, keeping them company when no one else was around.

The problem was, I didn't feel that way. Not very often anyway. Sure, there were moments when I felt especially connected to God in some way, but most of the time, I felt like I was stumbling around in the fog, feeling my way one cautious step at a time. I went to church every week; I had done church camp; I had brought more kids to our youth group and memorized more Bible verses than anyone else.

So what the hell was wrong with me?

Then the songs seemed to change. Maybe it was only me that changed, but the message of constant, irrepressible joy and praise gave way to a kind of arrogance that was palpable. There were songs about sitting at Jesus' right hand, and about courts, kingdoms, palaces, lords and such. And more and more, all of the blood and sacrifice language started working its way back in. But there was one song in particular that stood out above all the rest:

Our God is an awesome God
He reigns from heaven above
With wisdom, power, and love
Our God is an awesome God

Granted, they said "love" instead of "blood,' which was a plus, but I wasn't sure what the rest of it was supposed to mean. Our God? Seriously? Did we get a certificate of ownership when becoming a

Christian that I missed out on? The way these songs went on about how amazing and fantastic God was, He sounded like the next fancy laundry detergent or the latest sports car to roll off the line.

This God was awesome. He'd make my teeth white, my step straighter. I'd be happy all of the time, and man, wouldn't everyone who didn't have their God certificate be jealous?

The best cultural commentary on the absurdity of contemporary Christian praise music came from an episode of *Southpark*, where the kids were trying to make it big as a boy band. They weren't having any luck, given that they lacked the necessary talent to actually hit it big. But then Cartman stumbled upon a moment of clarity. He figured out that most of the Christian songs sounded just like mediocre romantic pop songs, except where the pop song said "baby," the Christians said "Jesus." Plus, he explained to the other boys, the Christian audiences clearly didn't mind if you lacked talent.

Jesus is my boyfriend. He's there for me when I'm feeling down. He tells me he loves me. He takes me to the movies and buys me popcorn. He always says please, thank you, and never forgets to put the toilet seat back down. And even if we're not sure we believe it, by the forty-seventh chorus of the same song in a row, it'll be burned into our cortexes for good. Like the old saying goes: fake it till you make it. Ir in this case, sing it till you believe it.

Isn't our God awesome?

A-B-C: Anything But Christian

I wasn't feeling the "Jesus boyfriend" vibe, so clearly I wasn't doing it right. Plus I was not ingratiating myself to my youth leaders with the incessant questions. Following the Bible-throwing incident, I walked away from the Christian faith for a decade. When I got to college, the only face of Christianity I saw on campus was the guy in snakeskin boots and a straw hat who literally stood on a box in the middle of the student union courtyard every Wednesday and yelled at us passersby through a bullhorn about the many and horrifying ways we were damning our souls to hell. People shouted challenges back at him or taunted him relentlessly, but he didn't listen. He just kept going, venom and spit spraying from his mouth until he had run out of Christian epithets for the seas of heathens, wallowing around him on all sides.

No one, and I mean no one I knew went to church. I wouldn't have known where to go even if I had been looking. Not that I was. I still had a spiritual hunger but I was certain that if there was a place at all that might help satisfy my longing, it sure as hell wasn't Christianity.

I took classes on Buddhism and Confucianism. I read Aristotle, Heidegger and Nietzsche. I sat and talked with the Hare Krishnas on campus for hours. I devoured Emmanuel Swedenborg. I meditated. I visited Unitarian Universalist gatherings. I explored paganism, Islam and Judaism. I made a point, though, of not settling too long in any one place. Sure, most of the folks of other faiths I met were friendly and more than happy to talk about their religion. But so were most Christians when you first met them. I just wanted to make sure I had moved on before the shine wore off and they, too, figured out I was God's sworn enemy.

I found my community in music, but of a different kind. Though I was kind of an awkward, quiet teenager in high school, I discovered that college was fertile ground for personal reinvention. No one knew that I had been accused of being gay when I hung out too much with my best friend at the Baptist church camp. No one knew that I still had the Carmen cassettes stashed underneath my bed, not because I wanted to keep them, but because I was afraid of what might happen if I threw away a Christian record. They didn't know I was a virgin, or that I hadn't kissed a girl until age sixteen, or that I had turned my back on the church.

I was Christian, the rock star.

Maybe "rock star" is overstating it a little, but I spent several wonderful years fronting rock bands around Texas. We'd belt out Alice in Chains, Tool, Soundgarden and all of the great grunge metal the nineties produced, straight from the angsty veins of the Pacific Northwest. Yes, this music was dark and even a little bloody at times. But it was supposed to be. It didn't pretend to be anything but visceral, powerful, angry.

I loved it.

I also didn't mind the free drinks people would set up on stage for me, or line up along the bar for us between sets. Lots of them. Oh, and as a virgin coming into college, I took care of that in short order upon arrival. The girls were free, liberated, aggressive even, and it turns out they really liked long haired guys who sang for rock bands and could get them on the list at their favorite clubs.

For the first time in my life, I was a badass. People told me I was awesome, and I was all too ready to agree with them. The more boisterous and obnoxious I got, the more people loved it. I never achieved any of the mythical stories first-hand about rockers trashing their dressing rooms because they were given the wrong color M&Ms, but I could see where that kind of radical behavior came from. People wanted you to be bigger than life. They wanted something to worship, and if the Christians wouldn't take us, we'd just create our own religion. And I was happy to be their god for the night.

If I said the drugs, alcohol, sex and clubbing weren't fun, I'd be lying. But it took its toll. There was the time I woke up just before noon to the phone ringing. It was my friend's apartment building, calling to inquire about an accident I'd apparently had during the night with their security gate. I denied it, of course, at least until they noted that they had my front license plate in their possession. Sure enough, I poked my head out the window and squinted at the front of my car: no license plate.

Then there was the incident with the stairs. I'd had one too many (maybe more than one) and had crashed over at a friend's house after a show. I remembered everything up to the point at which we ordered a round of Goldschlager shots for last call; after that, everything was a blur.

I woke up on the couch the next morning with a pounding headache, stains on my shirt and some crusted blood in a jagged trail along my temple. I tried to sit up, but the room spun violently causing me to ease myself back onto the cushions. According to my friend, I had wandered upstairs looking for God-knows-what. Upon returning to the top to the stairs, I slipped, falling about twenty-five stairs, head over feet, until smacking my head on the tile by the front door. The gash on my forehead opened up until a constant stream of blood flowed to the floor. And then I puked.

They realized I had probably given myself a bad concussion, as my pupils were completely out of whack. The blood seeping from the cut on my head showed no signs of slowing, and so they began to usher me out to the car to get me to the closest emergency room. Apparently I begged them not to, saying over and over again, "My mom will kill me...."

The gigs with my various bands eventually dried up, and I came to realize that my body was advancing in years far more rapidly than the calendar. Finally I got tired of waking up every day–often times not before noon–and feeling so old, so used up and wrung out. I got tired of forgetting what I'd done the night before or how I got home. I got tired of waking up next to someone whose name I couldn't remember. God knows I got tired of going to the doctor to get checked.

But mostly, I was just tired.

My life began to slow down, mostly as a means of survival if nothing else, but I still wanted nothing to do with God or church. If anything, my recent history only confirmed all the things I had been told about who I was: an apostate, an outcast, one of the Great Unwashed. But the scar tissue had built up over those old wounds through the years to the point that it didn't hurt so much any more when the voices in my head condemned me to hell for the millionth time. Either I grew deaf to them or they finally stopped.

And then, nothing.

Drop the Mic

A friend of mine, Trey, started a band years ago called "Everyday

Sunday" that was pretty huge in the Contemporary Christian Music scene (or CCM as they call it). They won awards, toured the world, played to sold-out crowds in stadiums and sold tens of thousands of records. It's not that often that you meet someone who can make a full-time living at music.

But he was also growing tired of the whole scene. It wasn't that he didn't want to play music anymore or was tired of his fans. Rather, he was part of the CCM tribe, which was effectively run and controlled by a very small handful of media executives who handled the flow of money, distribution of records, tour schedules, festival dockets...the whole nine yards. If you wanted to succeed in the CCM scene you had to work with them. And they had certain expectations about what your music would sound like, who you would play with, who would record your stuff, and even what was acceptable in your lyrics and what didn't pass muster.

They were always watching too. Trey said it was to the point that, if this drummer or that singer went out and had too much fun on Saturday night, he might get un-invited to perform on Sunday. But it went deeper than that.

"It got to the point," he says, "that I'd wonder to myself, 'Can I question this? Am I allowed to question this?' I mean, I don't know what I believe. Is it OK to say, 'I don't know what I think about this'? Can you say, 'I could be wrong, but here's what I think from my experience.'?

"Sometimes it would be nice to stop worrying all the time. Saying, 'I'm for this,' or 'I'm against this.' Those things are important at certain times and good to talk about, but if you could put it aside sometimes and not have to feel like you have to be right about this or that to be at our church, or a part of this festival or, you know, even be accepted into this music genre...if you could put all of those aside and just focused on what Jesus said about loving God and loving people, would that be good enough?"

"When you come to one of these big (Christian events), there are certain things that are acceptable, and certain things that aren't" says Trey. "A few things are assumed, like, 'we all know you have to accept Jesus to get into heaven,' and 'we're all against homosexuality,' and if you step outside of that mold...I mean look at what happened to Rob Bell."

One of the youngest of the big evangelical preachers, Rob was young, charismatic and he had a huge following. Aside from his church outside of Grand Rapids, Michigan, he had a devoted online audience. They were media savvy and educated, but more appealing to the religious establishment; they were young. Young people and families are the Holy Grail of nearly any church because they represent stability, growth and hopefully a sustainable stream of income for the Church to depend on into the future. And when the average age of a churchgoing person in the U.S. is over 60 and far fewer than 6% of Christian churches are growing[1], a pastor who can attract tens of thousands, if not hundreds of thousands, of young adults and families to their ministry is a rock star. They can basically write their own ticket.

That is unless they challenge the untouchables, like Rob did.

Rob Bell got away with a certain degree of unorthodox thinking because of his influence, but once he began to question the Christian position on LGBTQ people, there were big ripples. Then when his book, "Love Wins," came out in 2011, that was it. In it, he suggested that if there even was a hell, that a loving, gracious God would not condemn God's own creation to eternal conscious torment for all eternity. So by his reasoning, if hell was real, it would likely be empty.

Soon after, Rob was no longer pastor of Mars Hill, and he left congregational ministry all together. Never mind that his book hit the *New York Times* bestseller list and made the cover of *TIME Magazine*; he had tipped over a sacred cow.

"I don't think some people who may be more open minded understand what it's like to grow up in a family where you're told, 'This is the Word of God. Sure we've found ways to explain away being against slavery (Baptist preachers in the south opposed emancipation and told black people to accept their place in society), and women don't have to cover their heads in worship anymore (some churches still require it)...we've explained these things within the context of the culture, but the gay thing, not this. And even if you have questions about it, you don't fit."

After four albums, several number one hits and quite a bit of personal growth, Trey began to look deeper at his own industry. "I started to look at how it all works, where the money came from who's supporting it and who it's impacting. And it got me wondering if this was what I signed up for. Am I playing the game and doing what I know I the easiest way to make money, or am I making decisions based on where my heart is and what kind of person I want to be? All these questions started to filter in."

"I've supported Christian music for many years," he says, "and as for Christians coming together and asking how they can impact peoples' lives, I think that's a wonderful thing." But over time, within the CCM system, he felt like he was becoming "part of the problem." He still sang music that expressed how he felt about God and what mattered to him, but it troubled him to see how "all that was getting twisted. To see behind closed doors..." he says, "there are those who aren't saying what they really want to say, but they're using what the writers in Nashville will get them on radio. That's what the labels are doing, and that's what a lot of artists are saying. Then there's someone like Derek Webb (from Caedmon's Call) who has a different voice and is raising different kinds of questions, he's not going to get the time of day from Christian radio stations, which are supported by Christian communities who all know we're not supposed to ask those kinds of questions. And that cannot be a part of our voice as the church.

"Look at the top 40 charts," Trey says. "nobody sets out saying, 'man, I really want to be a contemporary Christian music artist. But then in the Christian music scene, that's exactly what's happening..." because of the tight controls, and because there is a strict formula from which artists are not allowed to stray. The result is derivative, watered-down iterations of whatever is trending at the time, all with the same handful of musicians, producers, engineers, record labels and radio stations pushing it out to the public.

After many years of being inside the subculture of contemporary Christian music, the message–rife with cliches and formulaic messaging–rang increasingly hollow. As Trey saw that those behind the scenes lived in ways that hardly reflected the values of the music they promoted, the facade he had believed in gradually began to crumble, until there was nothing left but a lie. He still loved his music, he loved God and he was still committed to using the former to express the latter. There just seemed to be no room left for him to do it within the CCM tribe.

"Maybe it's okay," he told me in our interview, "just to love somebody like you love yourself, you know? Maybe Jesus actually had something there."

But just because it was good enough for Jesus doesn't mean it was good enough for the contemporary Christian music industry. Trey and his band were out. We have since talked about the sense of being pushed out of what we had thought was our extended family. It's like being a spiritual orphan, with nowhere to go and much of your identity stripped away. In some ways such a paring down can be a good thing, leading us to question outside of culturally accepted norms who we are, what we believe and stand for.

But at the time, it's just scary as hell.

A Little Light Breaks In

My mom could hardly believe it when I called to tell her I'd met a girl. Not just any girl, but a minister. A Christian one.

"I think she's part of the Church of Christ," I said.

"I'm pretty sure they don't let women be ministers," said my mom.

"Ah. Probably not that then."

"So what are you going to do about the whole church thing?"

"I don't know," I said, "but I really like her, mom. This one's different."

It was awkward for a while, every time Amy would get ready to go to some churchy thing. I'd pretend to be really engrossed in a book or trying to catch up on work, but she'd always offer.

"You want to come with me?"

"I don't think so, thanks."

"Any reason?"

"Church and I just don't mix."

Finally, I realized that Amy wasn't going to let this one alone. I'd have to at least go with her one time in order to prove to her that I didn't belong there. One Sunday evening, I finally conceded, joking all the way there about the walls bursting into flames upon my arrival.

"I think you may be surprised," she said. "There's a whole lot of people there like you, with a similar story." I had been told by everyone under the sun that their church was different. It was kind of like when you tried to tell someone you hate fish, but they'd insist you just hadn't had any really good fish. So you try their fish, you hate it, and they look at you like you're the freak for not liking the fish.

I told you I hated the fish. So stop trying to give me fish already.

But Amy's group of friends was kind of different. They all sat in a circle, and no one was dressed in a suit. No one asked me if Jesus was my personal lord and savior, or if I knew where I'd go when I died. After the service, we all went around the corner for dinner at the Hornet, and several people–the preacher included–ordered a *beer*. They were just people, who also happened to have a love of this Jesus guy in common. And if I was being honest, it never was Jesus that I had the big problem with.

It was Christians.

These folks didn't strike me as Christians, though, at least according to the stereotypes I carried around in my head to kick around whenever I was made to feel like less of a person by one of Christ's chosen. Sure, these folks weren't perfect, but they seemed…real. It was a new experience, so I agreed to come back for one more week, figuring the veneer would have worn off and their true Christian colors eventually would come shining through.

The second shoe never dropped, so I kept coming, if for no other reason than to stay in good graces with Amy. I was always on guard, though, ready to be disappointed, certain that they would all let me down like everyone else. I was a prisoner of my own anti-Christian pride and I didn't even realize it.

"I hear you're a musician," said Paul, after offering that evening's message.

"Uhh, well," I hedged, "probably not like what you're thinking, no."

"What do you mean?"

"I mean, I don't sing any songs about Jesus."

"That's okay," he smiled. "Let's keep talking a little. Walk with me." He asked me if I'd be willing to play a couple of songs in next week's service. Just something that was meaningful to me. He assured me they didn't have to have the words "glory," "worship" or "savior" anywhere in them. He just wanted to make a space for me to share something that mattered to me, with the hope that it might matter to someone else too.

The following Sunday, I thought I was going to throw up before worship started. I was sure I'd make an idiot of myself, though Amy, clearly sensitive to my nerves, assured me whatever happened would be great. Sounds like something you'd say to your six-year-old before they get up on stage to play "London Bridge" on the recorder at a school talent show. But I had said I'd do it, and asshole or not, I did what I said I'd do.

My hands were shaking when I started the first song, but fortunately I had anticipated this and had picked a song that was only strumming and no finger-picking. I closed my eyes and tried to remember to breathe.

And then it happened. My voice began to shake, followed by a tear, edging toward the corner of my eye. Before I got halfway through the first chorus, I was a sobbing mess. I'm not exactly what you might call a weepy person; I usually cry out of basic human obligation once every four years or so, just to make sure I'm still alive. And I definitely don't cry in front of other people. Yet here I was, blubbering like an idiot in the middle of church, in front of my girlfriend and a couple dozen other people I hardly knew.

"Excuse me," I said, and walked out. Amy followed me, placing her hand on my back as I let the waterworks fly.

"It's okay," she said. "It's really okay."

"No, it's not okay," I said, kicking the stone in the walls of the corridor. "I looked like a frigging idiot in there. I made a total ass of myself. Plus I didn't even finish the song."

"They understand," she said. "Trust me, if any group gets where you're at, it's this one. Plus you can try again with the second song."

"Umm, no," I laughed, sniffling and wiping my nose. "I think I'm done."

"Come on," she nudged me back toward the circle in the main room, "it'll be okay." But it wasn't. A dozen measures into the next song I started braying like a jackass again, but this time

I just sat there and cried. Hell, they'd already seen me do it once. Why try to hide it? They already knew I was a mess, and there was no way to gloss over that now. But one after another, they offered their thanks to me, sharing a hug, a pat on the shoulder or a smile.

"That was pretty brave, what you did in there," said Paul. "I really admire that."

"Brave, right," I sighed. "Sorry I screwed up your service."

"Actually," he said, "I don't think we've worshipped like that in a long, long time. Thank you."

Wait. Me, help people worship? Was he insane? All I did was squawk out a few notes then blow snot bubbles all over the place. How could that possibly be worship? But once I got over the initial embarrassment, I started to understand a little bit. Something had opened up in me, just a little, but enough. When I put the guitar in my hands and gave my music over to something bigger than myself, all of the scar tissue I'd been building up for ten years couldn't hold up. I was broken open, asshole and all, and it was beautiful.

Messy, totally off pitch and kind of snotty, but beautiful.

Ironically, in reacting against the asshole-ish attitudes I had encountered previously, I ended but being a bit of a judgmental asshole myself. I didn't trust that they were different than what I knew (I had heard this way too many times before) and I was jaded. But at the heart of it, it was because of the hurt I still carried around.

I'll always be grateful for a handful of beer-loving folks for introducing me to a new perspective on a faith I had written off as lost to me. But more than that, I'm glad Amy was just enough more stubborn than I was to get me to work through my own fear and judgment. And lucky for me, what I found on the other side of that was something I had missed for far too long.

BUILD YOUR OWN CONTEMPORARY CHRISTIAN SONG!

See if Cartman's formula works for you. Pick lyrics for the list of songs below, or find your own. Then do a holy remix.

Replace any references to "you," "man," "woman," "boy" or "girl" with:

- God
- Jesus
- Lord
- King
- Savior
- Prince
- Spirit
- Redeemer
- Baby Jesus (extra points for this one)
- Father (can be pretty creepy if placed properly)

Optional - replace other random nouns with:

- Kingdom
- Throne
- Sin
- Judgement
- Rapture
- Gates (gilded, of course)
- Palace
- Warrior
- Angel (archangel is a bonus)
- Cherubim
- Faith
- Seraphim
- Grace
- Apocalypse (not in many CCM songs, but hey, it's fun!)

Take any verbs out (especially any naughty ones) and replace them with one of the following:

- Worship
- Praise
- Pray
- Save
- Rejoice
- Adore
- Serve
- Sanctify
- Kneel
- Bow
- Evangelize
- Hath
- Proclaim
- Soar
- Doth
- Reign/Reigneth

Remove adjectives and put in some of these:

- Glorious
- Wondrous
- Holy
- Amazing
- Perfect
- Born again
- Renewed
- Shining
- Redeemed
- Mighty
- Almighty (always better than mighty)
- Great
- Awesome
- Golden

Then sprinkle a few of these in here and there at the ends of phrases, just for color. And it doesn't really matter if you don't know what they mean; most Christians don't really know either:

- Hallelujah
- Maranatha
- Hosanna
- Amen
- The end is near (not really a praise phrase, but a fun one regardless)
- ...for Jesus*

*It turns out that you can do almost anything you want, as long as you add "for Jesus" at the end. Take "baby, I want you." Change it to "Baby I want you...for Jesus." I smell a hit!

4

OUR A**HOLE LEGACY

Amy has a hard job, and I know I don't want it. There were about five minutes one day when I thought I did, but I really don't.

When she went to seminary, I started absorbing the ideas through her and our friends, all of who were "church nerds." Little did I realize how fascinating I would find theology. I enjoyed philosophy in college, and my graduate work in psychology was really fulfilling. But something about theology brought them both together. There was the abstract, esoteric nature of thinking and talking about something that can't ever really be named, or even proven to exist. For a navel gazer like me, that's actually a fun kind of challenge. Then in the context of church, or even just when someone is in crisis, all of the talking, reading and thinking has to kick into practical gear.

Amy's great at that part. I'm not. And honestly, I don't even want to be. Some days I'm not even sure I like people on the whole enough to dedicate my life to serving them the way she does. I mean, I do a lot of writing and speaking about the larger ideas surrounding social justice, the changing face and future of organized religion... big picture nerdy shit. But when it comes to actually *helping people*, day after day, I'm glad to hand that over to Rev. Amy.

I know it's kind of an asshole confession to admit that, even though my work strives to be deeply personal and affecting, I'm not a big "people fan." But there it is. You already knew I'm an asshole, so what's the point in obfuscating?

I love writing and thinking *about* people, while Amy really loves people because...well, I guess you'd have to ask her why. For me, I tend to set expectations for the human race so high that they're rarely realistic, and yet I never seem to learn from the letdown when folks can't measure up to my imaginary universe.

Trust me: if they could, that place would be awesome.

I've actually taken a step back from church. After more than fifteen years of doing church with her, I'm more than a little burned out. Over and over again, I bump up against the reality that church brings out both the best and worst in people. And when it's the latter, I tend to reciprocate, especially when I'm short on patience. So I'm taking a few months off.

My sabbatical was well timed too, because the second week I went down to the coffee shop to write instead of be a big, fat Jesus head, we had some visitors at church. I should explain that we are at a historic 136-year-old church in the heart of downtown Portland. There was a time when urban living was on a downward slide that the congregation considered selling their valuable property and relocating out in the suburbs. Ultimately, they agreed to stick with urban ministry. And in Portland, that means life can get pretty interesting.

We've had guys on meth or drunk out of their minds bring worship to a grinding halt. Turns out, in addition to teaching classes, leading beer and hymns (yes, really) and organizing young adult stuff, I became a *de facto* bouncer when necessary. There was the time that my son, Mattias, came out of the bathroom during a community barbecue and told me there was a guy acting weird in one of the stalls. Actually, he was masturbating, which is definitely weird, but more scary and creepy than anything, especially with my kid in there.

We find used needles, broken glass and dirty underwear in the gardens. Just this week, Amy had to run off a couple who decided to give baby-making a go in our courtyard. The guy was even taking pictures, as if eyewitness statements to police wasn't incriminating enough. We accommodate schizophrenics, bipolar travelers and a host of other unique characters, which is part of having a fairly open-door policy right next to the park with the most homeless squatters in the city.

But none of it compares to the assholes I was fortunate enough to miss this particular Sunday.

I should probably explain a few things that led up to this incident. First, not long after we got to town, Amy decided we needed to do something to show people in the community we were different and actually meant what we said about love, openness, compassion and the like. The very fact that people tend not to believe religious rhetoric in itself is a problem, but one that can be dealt with by living differently. And sometimes, it takes creativity.

I've written before about this, but in case you don't catch every blog post, I'll recap. There was a gay pride festival happening down by the waterfront, and we agreed we should go down there as a family. But then Amy had the idea of creating a big sandwich board and wearing it not just at the festival, but all the way from the church to the festival and back too. The sign says something like "As a Christian, I'm sorry for all the times you've been excluded, shamed or marginalized in the name of God."

It got a lot of attention, and to my pleasant surprise, people were incredibly grateful and gracious. So she decided to keep the sign in her window, which faces Park Avenue. You could say it's not exactly subtle; I actually love watching people glance at it as they walk by, only to freeze in place and read it two or three times, just to make sure they're reading it right.

Christians, apologizing? I can almost hear them thinking to themselves. *Now that's actually kinda cool.* Or at least to some people it is, but definitely not our special visitors that Sunday. They decided to take her apology personally, as if her act of humility was an affront not just to Christianity in general, but to them in particular. Never mind she hadn't ever met them before. It was all about them. And it pissed them off.

Then there was the fact that our church recently went public as an "open and affirming" church, which means that we welcome LGBTQ people just as we would anyone else. They can worship with us, serve as leaders, be employees, or even pastor the church. Granted, we were already a pretty open and welcoming church before this, but back to the whole "action, not words" thing, some people need a sign that we're going out of our way to be welcoming. After all, how many church signs have you seen with the words "ALL ARE WELCOME" on it? And how many times have you thought to yourself, "I'm the asterisk at the end of that welcome."? I know I have. I expect there to be a scroll of fine print that unrolls if you get closer that lays out those groups who are exempt from welcome, or the conditions under which you can be worthy of inclusion.

In short, the whole "ALL ARE WELCOME" thing sounds nice, but most of us are pretty sure it's bullsh**.

On top of the sign that clearly was about making fun of five guys we'd never met rather than trying to make things right with a traditionally marginalized group of people, and then We went official as an open and affirming church, There's the whole boobs thing. Personally, I'm a big fan of Amy having boobs, among other things. But for some, once you put said boobs behind a pulpit, that's just going too far.

As my friend back in Texas used to say though, if you're using your penis to preach, you're doing it wrong.

These five guys came just before worship this particular Sunday to offer their disapproval about what we stood for as representatives of Christianity. And yes, they had the red-faced screaming thing and the "burn in hell" sandwich boards, and by God, they were on a mission to set us right. They kept yelling and carrying on at the foot of the church steps about how we were leading people down the slippery slope to doom, and about how we were all "fag lovers" and sodomites, grinding our thumb in the eye of the Almighty.

As usually happens with guys like this, they started to draw a crowd. Even some of the guys who live in the park came over and told them to chill out and let our folks worship. Now, when the guys who use the side of your building as a toilet are telling your detractors to bring it down a few notches, you feel you're really getting somewhere.

Now, I only know what happened in such detail because someone had their phone recording the whole thing, just in case they got violent. The police even came by, but free speech laws in Oregon are really liberal; as long as they were on the sidewalk, weren't defacing property and weren't getting violent, they were free to be as obnoxiously hateful as they wanted.

A few of our folks came out and tried talking to them, to no avail. But they had saved the best for Amy. The real kicker was when they made it personal. "God," one of the red-faced protesters bellowed, "I pray for you to strike this woman. Kill this woman in your righteous judgment!" And he didn't stop there. "God, send her children straight to hell, before they do the same to others with their abominable heresies!"

Ok, asshole, now it's on. Like I said, ultimately I was glad I wasn't there, because I'm afraid someone would have gone to the hospital and I would have ended up in jail. Yeah, I know, not the Christ-like response, but praying for my wife's death and for my children to burn in hell found my soft spot.

Just as bad–or maybe even worse–were the after-effects. Amy would cry spontaneously for several days afterward. She was scared to go to her office, exposed to the park blocks through her big picture window. She even warned our kids not to answer the door without an adult with them, and told them to stay away from windows. They had threatened to come to some of our houses and continue terrorizing us, so she wasn't just overreacting. If their goal was to scare and intimidate, it worked.

How in the hell did we go from the life and teaching of a man two thousand years ago who believed so fervently in his message of peacemaking, humble service and compassion, to scaring women and children half to death? How can we even call these two things even remotely related? Something went wrong; something was horribly broken. But what? And when?

* * *

Christians acting like assholes has a long, storied history. But since this isn't a history book, I'll try to distill some critical turning points in the Christian story down to five things. First on the list was a big one, and man, did it get ugly.

The First Christian Empire

During the time of Jesus, the territory where Jewish tribes lived was occupied by the Roman Empire. In fact, the Romans controlled a hefty chunk of that piece of the world. They led with a sort of benevolent dictatorship called the *pax Romana*. This meant that you and your peeps would be taken care of, so long as you didn't stir things up too much. If you did...well, we all know what happened to Jesus for causing trouble.

So as Christianity spread after Jesus' death, it was really just in little pockets, and it was generally in secret. They even used code to communicate, like the annoying fish you see on the back of Chevy pickups or in ads for plumbers. It used to be that one guy would draw an arc in the sand with a stick. If the other guy drew an opposing arc, making a little fishy out of it (called an *ichthus),* then they knew they were both Christians. It was a kind of secret handshake, all while endeavoring to keep their heads attached to their shoulders.

But the Christian underground movement kept spreading, and it was starting to become bothersome for Constantine, the emperor at the time. He wanted to keep all of his territories in line, and even expand Roman reach. But he would need a partner to make it work. That's when he decided he would make Christianity the official religion of the Roman Empire. It was the first theocracy of its kind, marrying church and state in a way that was of great mutual benefit to both.

Not such a good deal for non-Christians, or for those who didn't do it right. But oh well...

Speaking of which, Constantine realized that there were lots of different ways people were practicing Christianity, and it was pretty hard to manage. So he convened the Council of Nicea, and they drew up the Nicene Creed: sort of the "pledge of allegiance" for all Christians to follow. Or else.

Actually, Constantine wasn't as fierce of a tyrant about Christianity as he's blamed for sometimes. The marriage of convenience was far more about strategy than ideology. It was Charlemagne, who came along after Constantine, who was the zealot. And when ferocious ideology is backed by the biggest power in the world, things get bloody.

The good news for Christianity on the whole was that this theocratic juggernaut was the key to spreading the faith all across the world. The bad news, especially for indigenous people around the planet met by Roman forces, was that they had to become Christians or die. It's what I call the "assimilate or exterminate" approach, and of course it was justified by the fact that their eternal salvation was at stake. So converting them to the one-true faith was paramount; make them see the light at all costs, even if it meant slaughtering people by the tens of thousands in the process.

So that happened.

The Almighty Brain

So this kind of church-plus-state dominance is in our cultural DNA, but of course, that doesn't make it okay. We'll get to how that came to fruition specifically in the United States, but first, let's blame the Enlightenment for some stuff.

On the whole, the Enlightenment period was pretty great for everything from commerce to philosophy, the arts and an overall paradigm shift in the way we think of ourselves. It started more or less with these guys getting together in coffeehouses around Europe who would catch up on current news, debate about politics and ideas, and even do a deal or two. The modern-day stock market has the Enlightenment to thank for its beginnings, and some of our greatest artwork exploded out of the Enlightenment Period.

But while there was a lot of intellectual and cultural advancement we got from it, there were also some tricky side effects. For one, we began to celebrate the sacred art of mental masturbation. We elevated human logic to an almost godlike status. Post-Enlightenment liberal though basically argued that literally *everything* could be understood, argued and explained through human logic. That even included God.

The other thing that happened along with this was an embrace of the idea of clear lines of right and wrong, good and bad, in and out: a kind of dualist thinking that had its roots all the way back in Plato, but now it took mystery and the idea of the coexistence of multiple truths and gave it an atomic wedgie, took its lunch money and stuck its head in the toilet.

This kind of modernist thought even worked its way into the Church. That mentality that sheep go to heaven and goats go to hell—and of course you can't be a little of both—had its religious history in the "proto-orthodoxy" set in motion by Constantine. But now we used this intellectual tool to stake even bolder claims about everything from the mind of God to how many angels could fit on the head of a pin. And of course there had to be a winner and a loser; there was no room for "maybe."

Our spiritual heritage of "mysticism" that reached as far back as pre-Christian Judaism was seen as weak and anemic, or even heretical. And once Martin Luther came along and broke away from the Catholics, kicking off the Protestant Reformation, that ephemeral, contemplative stuff was way too Catholic anyway. So it was pretty much out.

Plundering for Jesus

The first thing we think of when we talk about Manifest Destiny probably isn't Christianity, but they're at least good cousins. In case you snoozed during that seventh-grade history lesson, Manifest Destiny was a belief that took hold during the expansion and establishment of Anglo settlements west and south, stretching colonial influence from coast to coast. The idea wasn't just that we were able to take over the land; we were, in fact *destined* to do it. Now, on the surface it wasn't an inherently God-ordained sort of destiny. It was actually based principally on Darwinian teaching, believe it or not. The idea that the white settlers actually were a more evolved subspecies of human than the indigenous savages (translated: brown people), so they were actually doing them a favor by bringing their superior civilization into the midst of these lesser people.

This was complementary to the Christian mission in a way. As an example, founders and early leaders of the Mormon faith (among others) correlated with the superiority of Anglos over indigenous people to scripture, claiming that people with darker skin bore the "mark of Cain." Cain, of course, was the first murderer in the Bible, and was described as being hairy and darker skinned. Never mind that most Native Americans have less facial and body hair than Anglos; it was justification enough to believe they were inferior.

Combine that with the fact that they were non-Christian, and that the primary mission of the faith was to convert the unsaved to the on-true faith, and you had a divine mandate to spread the Good Word, and at all costs. So in this way, the frontier evangelism pulled both from Manifest Destiny and the dualist thought that took hold after the Enlightenment. Now the immortal soul and its eternal fate was the most important thing: more important even than one's own dignity, well being, or even their life. And of course, those who refused to convert fell into the distinct category of "other," and were an inherent threat to God's mission.

This was all that was needed to fuel the "convert or die" mission of frontier Christians to relocate and slaughter native population of North America as they spread west. It also justified waging a sort of holy war against Mexico to the south, because all of it was being done in the name of the Christian God.

Jesus Was a Republican

Fast forward to the late 1970s, and there was growing concern within the leadership of the Christian Right that America was losing it's moral focus. Following the socio-political unrest of the late sixties and the fairly hedonistic self-indulgence that helped define the seventies, something needed to be done. And Baptist pastor Jerry Falwell was the man to make it happen.

Falwell and his cohorts helped establish an organization in 1979 called the Moral Majority that aimed to shift the cultural conversation back to a more righteous path. And this was not to be done through teaching or example, but rather with money and power. So the group set its sights on politics.

Throughout the 1980s, the political action committees under the umbrella of the Moral Majority raised millions of dollars and mobilized voters to usher in a revolution through the systems of power on both regional and national levels. In particular, they were instrumental in helping get Ronald Regan elected as president twice.

Technically, Falwell's organization was an interfaith group, given that there were at least symbolic representations in leadership by including one Jewish board member and a couple of Catholics. They also had at least loose ties with some Democrats. But in spirit, the alliance was distinctly between conservative Protestant and Republicans.

We don't really have to look any further than the primary areas of focus at the heart of the Moral Majority's mission to understand what they were about. Their focus, beyond getting the "right" people elected, was ultimately to reestablish an emphasis on traditional family values (at least as they defined them), opposition to abortion and homosexuality, discrediting the "liberal media," advocating for prayer in schools, and conversion to anyone and everyone to their strain of conservative, fundamentalist Christianity.

Suffice it to say that the Jewish guy, and probably the Catholics, weren't exactly thrilled about this last one in particular.

But the strategy worked, and the eighties saw a wave of conservatism sweep into capitol hill and state-level government. About a decade later, the organization's funding and organizing power started fading, but by then, they claimed victory in marrying conservative political agenda items with those of the right wing of the Christian Church.

And the marriage has been ongoing ever since.

Jesus and the Benjamins

It's weird to think that a movement based around a guy who died homeless and broke, and who told people to give what they had away led to the idea that he also wanted us to be rich. I wrote about the beginnings of what we now call Prosperity Gospel in my last book, *postChristian*, but in a nutshell it started with Oral Roberts in the 1940s giving birth to something he called "Seed Faith" ministry. From there, ministers like him started preaching the good news of personal prosperity, which lots of people liked. Not surprising really, since hearing that God wants us to be comfortable and rich is a hell of a lot better than struggling to let go of the control the material world has over us.

Basically, Prosperity Gospel reinforced the idea (as it still does today) that it's all about you. To put it more bluntly like how Gordon Gecko said it in the movie *Wall Street,* greed is good. We love being validated for who we already are and being told we don't really have to change. It's great to hear that money and faithfulness go together like peas and holy carrots. And for the poor, it offered them a way out; if they prayed hard enough, believed strongly enough and of course made a healthy donation to the church, they too could be lifted by Jesus himself out of their trial into the middle class and beyond.

Prosperity Gospel also was a beneficiary of excellent timing, attaching itself first to radio programs nationwide and then television. You couldn't turn on the TV or scan the FM dial without coming across another prosperity ministry, offering you a prayer cloth in exchange for a donation. The pastors got ridiculously rich, which of course was a testament to their faith, those who were affluent were justified both in not changing their priorities and even in pursuing more. Even the poor were offered a glimpse of breaking the poverty cycle, and, as we know, hope has no price tag.

After all, if they were poor, it must be because they aren't praying enough, right?

Loving Your Enemies Sucks

I confessed at the beginning of this chapter that I had far from Christlike inclinations toward these protesters, especially once they attacked my family. Then it was personal; Jesus would have to ride the bench on this one while I kick some ass. But we were fortunate on two counts; I wasn't around to lapse into asshole mode, and Amy not only didn't get hooks, but she even set an example in her response that inspired a lot of people.

"I had to really stop and consider what I was going to do when I went out there," she told me. "I went in my office and prayed about it. I knew I couldn't just ignore it, and I also couldn't just get into a shouting match with them." That is, after all, what they were hoping for, or even to evoke violence so they can then turn around and sue us and the whole church for assault.

Exactly why it was good I wasn't there.

Amy walked out to meet the protesters calmly and with a sincere smile on her face. You can tell she had made peace with them before she even stepped outside. She had someone bring water, coffee and cookies to them and tired to hand them out. "All that shouting has to make your throat dry," she said. "Would you like some water or a snack to keep your energy up?" One man kicked the bottle of water away that she set at his feet.

"I don't want your water," he growled. "I drink from living water!" She ignored his aggression and moved on. A few folks from church and the park were getting pulled in, so she turned to reassure and calm them down. Then she got to the last guy in the group and stood a couple of feet from him as he fumed and yelled horrible things in her face.

"I love you," she said in a calm, even tone, "I love you." She just kept repeating it over and over again, until he quieted down enough to hear what she was saying. "This isn't you," she continued. "I know there's more to you than this, and this isn't who you are. I love you." The young man blinked at her, silent and stunned. After a minute or so, he finally turned toward someone else and rattled off some more of his bile, but he never directed his aggression toward her again.

That alone is remarkable enough, but then a couple of hours later, after they all had left, that same young man came back to the church. He went inside and sought out our regional minister (which is kind of like a bishop but without any power and no pointy hats). "That pastor said she loved me before," he said quietly. "Did she mean it?"

"Yeah," he answered, "of course she does. We all do."

"Then will you help me?"

"What do you need?" he asked.

"I need $5,000 in dental work," said the young guy.

Now, I can't read minds, and I wasn't around to try and read his reaction. But if I was a betting man, I'd wager he was thinking something along the lines of *oh sh*t.* We don't exactly have $5,000 lying around in petty cash. But you can't tell someone you love him and then not be ready to back it up. After all, I've noted before that our respective gifts and values should be shared at every opportunity with the world, but that we should only use words to do it when absolutely necessary. Love is something you have to *do*, not just talk about.

We do have a retired dentist in our church, and we have helped a few guys who live outside get their dental work taken care of, between our guy and the public services we help people access. So it's not going to happen overnight, but if he was willing to be that vulnerable and come back to the church he was condemning and praying for God to burn to the ground and make himself vulnerable enough to ask for help, we sure as hell had better be ready to help.

I should also mention that a friend of mine and I blogged about the experience, and both went a little viral. Mine got picked up on *Huffington Post,* and a local news station saw one of our posts and called Amy for an interview. It ended up being the top news story that night on the 5 and 6 o'clock news. A few folks who saw what she did and admired it, and others from the LGBTQ community who appreciated our new stance on being an open and affirming community came to check us out too.

The newcomers may stay, or they may just be passing through out of curiosity. And the world still has plenty of examples of people who call themselves Christians being hateful, obnoxious, arrogant, fear-mongering assholes. And the protester who came back might use his new teeth to chew on some other church's ass for being too open, welcoming and loving. But at least in that moment, Amy made room for inspired love to interrupt the noise and hate for a few minutes. She did her part. She might even have inspired others to try and do a little better the next time they have a chance.

I know it inspired me, and gave me a glimmer of hope that we're doing something right, trying to live into the example offered by this Jesus guy.

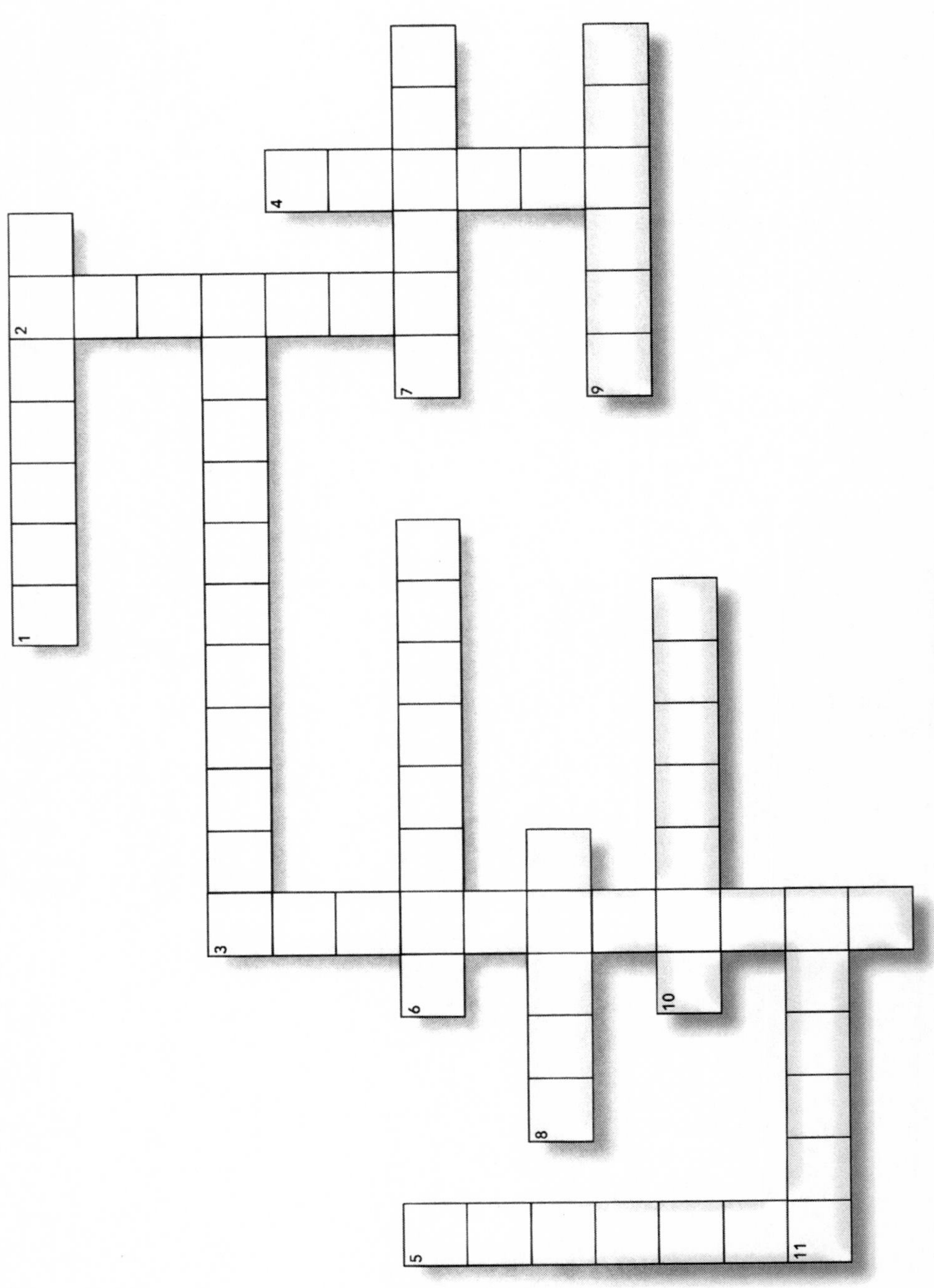
1
2
3
4
5
6
7
8
9
10
11

NAME THAT CHRISTIAN

Fill in the last names of the infamous christians throughout our history who have helped us become what we are today!

ACROSS

1 Colorado megachurch pastor busted for getting a handle from a male escort in a massage parlor.

3 Created the Nicene Creed and made Christianity a global imperial franchise.

6 Former Acts 29 preacher who once wrote an article about how women's genitalia were designed by God to be "penis houses."

7 Took prosperity gospel, added a blow dryer, perfect teeth and a gigantic stadium in Houston, TX to build his own empire.

8 Pastor once quoted as saying, "It's right for God to slaughter women and children anytime he pleases."

9 Focus on the Family founder who advocated spanking children as young as 18 months, and recommended using a hand, belt or paddle to discipline uppity kids.

10 Mad props for founding the Moral Majority and taking a dump on separation of church and state, buddy!

11 Former Word of Faith Texas prosperity preacher, also the subject of a viral "fart overdub" video because of the squinty faces he made when divinely inspired.

DOWN

2 Seed Faith ministry was the grandaddy of today's Prosperity Gospel.

3 Took his predecessor's Roman imperial plan and added a dash (or millions) of spilled blood.

4 Westboro Baptist founder who made hate a full-time ministry.

5 Says evolution is a "fairy tale for grown ups; a farce; intellectual-free zone; bogus science," and offers the banana as evidence of God and an earth only a few thousand years old.

Answers on the back!

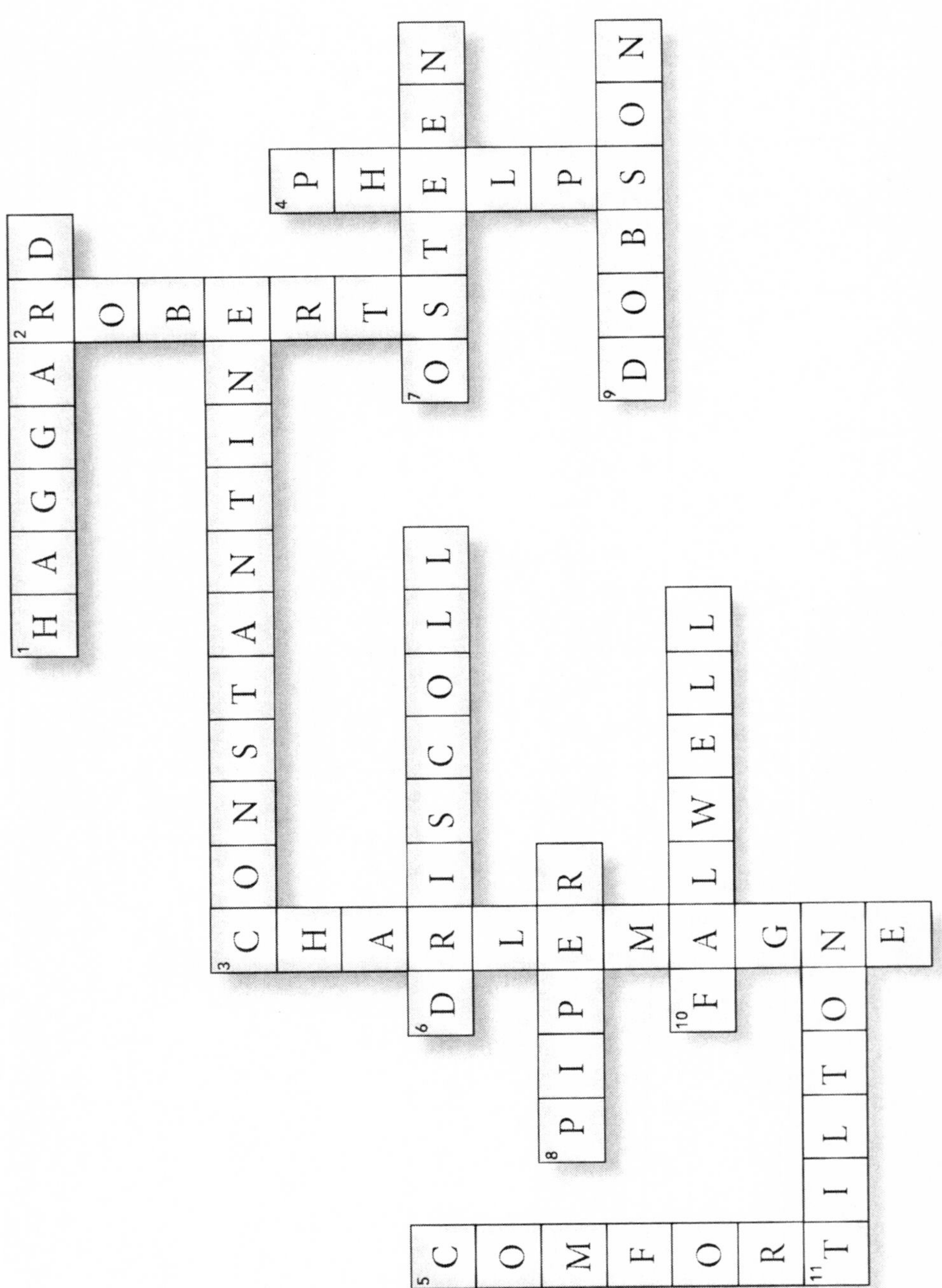
1 HAGGARD
2 ROBERTS
3 CONSTANTINE
3 CHARLEMAGNE
4 PHELPS
5 COMFORT
6 DRISCOLL
7 OSTEEN
8 PIPER
9 DOBSON
10 FALWELL
11 TILTON

BIBLE BEAT-DOWN

I've dropped some gems already that some folks' use in talking about the Bible that tend to shut down conversation. Unless you agree, of course; then it's all good! But since we're all friends here by now, I thought I'd dive into some of those infamous passages often used to exclude people, judge them, condemn who they are or even do violence against them. But before we can do that in a way that is most helpful, let's talk about what the Bible is in the first place.

I was just asked today by a student how it is I approach scripture, if not literally. After all, how do we keep from cherry-picking the bits we like and ignoring stuff that makes us uncomfortable? If I don't take everything in scripture exactly at its word, who's to say I'm not using it just to promote my own personal agenda? Maybe I'm co-opting these sacred texts and actually using them to lead people *away* from truth and from God, rather than closer to them.

Maybe so. God knows I've been accused of that, and a hell of a lot worse. Suffice it to say that when some people hear the phrase "asshole Christian," my face is the first thing that pops up in their mind. Maybe they even have a picture of me on their church dartboard, or paste copies of my head shot in the backs of the urinals for target practice.

Now that would be awesome. But I'm probably being grandiose.

Preacher, theologian and biblical scholar Fred Craddock once said that there is no such thing as uninterpreted scripture, and I think he's onto something. Consider the fact that language, by its very nature, is symbolic, which means it's *not the thing*. Unless you're a master calligrapher, the squiggles on the page aren't the point of writing; the whole purpose is to convey and idea, tell a story, evoke an emotion, state a case and so on. But as soon as you put pen to paper, you put your ideas through the sausage maker. You can't just download your idea in its pure form into someone else's cerebral cortex. And even though you might get really close to what you meant with just the right words, that doesn't mean the person reading it will get exactly the same meaning from them.

Yes, even if they take it "literally."

If it was that simple, we wouldn't need the Supreme Court to interpret the Constitution of the United States. For that matter, we shouldn't need preachers or Sunday School teachers to explain scripture to us either, since the literal, pure, perfect meaning would be sitting there, right in front of us.

So Craddock was right; even the most fervent Christian fundamentalist interprets scripture. And if they read the Bible in English, they're leaving translation and interpretation in the hands of other people. And if that process was perfect, we wouldn't need seven thousand different versions of the Bible, would we?

The Bible 101

Part of the issue begins in how we even approach the Bible. Sometimes we'll search through the pages (or Google, more likely) to find some passage that supports something we already think or believe. This is called *proof-texting* and although it's the cornerstone of many a modern ministry, it's a major no-no. My wife, Amy, says that you can make almost any point you want if you pull a particular piece of scripture out of context and squint at it just right. Oh, and yelling really loud about it and whacking your Bible on the table helps too.

We can use the Bible to justify keeping slaves. In fact, that's exactly what a contingency of Christians did in the south United

States before desegregation. And a solid chunk of Christians still use the Bible to keep some people out of leadership positions in church, including half of the species (sorry ladies). We could also use it to justify that no Bible-believing Christian should ever own anything, since Jesus told a rich man in the Gospels that to inherit God's kingdom, he had to sell everything he had and give it to the poor. There are other examples, but you get the idea. So we'll put the *kaibash* on proof-texting.

It's also tricky—even dangerous—to pick up the Bible with the intent of reading it all, start at page one and plow forward, one page at a time like it's a novel. These texts never were written with that in mind. It's not a Die Hard script. It doesn't have some linear, neat and clean beginning, middle and ending to it. Some of the books are poetry or song lyrics, while others are laws or social rules. Then there's a lot of history, genealogy and so forth, and it wasn't assembled into what we now call the Bible until centuries after it was all finished.

So yeah, Jesus didn't have a Bible lying around. He was Jewish anyway, you know. They studied from the *Talmud,* part of which is in the Bible. But it's not the whole thing. The *Talmud* is made up of both written and oral scriptures. The first five books of the Christian Bible (also called the "Pentateuch") are part of the *Talmud*. By itself, it's called the *Torah*.

I know I'm a Bible geek, but we've got to have some kind of understanding of how the Bible works. Grab have a beer.

So the Bible isn't a novel. It's not an adventure story where the Christians reign supreme and everyone else gets to suck it. Granted, there are still a healthy number of Christians out there who believe this, and they probably won't appreciate my saying so. But I think the idea that "Christians win" not only is damaging and twisted; it's diametrically opposed to the kind of world Jesus was talking about his entire ministry.

Silly humans.

For me, this is a helpful way to think about the Bible. First, it was written in three different languages: Hebrew, Aramaic and Greek. Nearly the entire Old Testament was written in Hebrew, the spoken and written language of the Jewish people. Only the books attributed to the prophets Ezra and Daniel, and one single verse in the book of Jeremiah (don't ask) were written in Aramaic, which technically isn't a language, distinct from the Hebrew. Instead it's a family of languages used by the Jewish people, which included Hebrew, Canaanite and Phoenician languages. Jews were a nomadic culture, so they picked up lots of bits and pieces from surrounding cultures, along with their languages. So Aramaic is kind of an umbrella terms for the languages and dialects they used.

For Protestants (Christians who don't identify as Catholic), the Old Testament is made up of 39 books, written over one thousand years. Think about that! And some of these stories were passed on verbally for generations before ever being written down. Lots of people back then weren't literate and couldn't read or write. So the main way to share information was orally. Catholics, on the other hand, include seven more books in their Old Testament, which by themselves are called the Apocrypha. Most Protestants don't recognize these as part of the Bible, though the Catholic Church does.

See, we can't even agree on how many books are in the Bible!

Also, from now on, when I talk about the Old Testament, I'm going to call it the Hebrew Bible, which is pretty common among Bible nerds. This is mainly because Jewish people don't always take too kindly to us suggesting that their sacred texts are the old, incomplete ones, and we came along, adding the "new and improved" parts.

That's the Hebrew Bible. Then there's the New Testament which is, in fact, chronologically newer than the previous 39 books (or 46 if you're Catholic). The New Testament is 27 books all together, starting with the Gospels. This actually means "good news," mainly because it tells about the life, teaching and ministry of Jesus. For some, the *real* good news is that Jesus died for your sins, so they can't wait to get to the dead Jesus parts. Personally, I'm more a fan of the alive parts.

The Gospels are the first four books of the New Testament together. This is where a lot of the "greatest hits" come from. Most people who know nothing else about the Bible know that the Gospels are made up of books attributed to Matthew, Mark, Luke and John. But you'd think that would mean that this was the order they were written in, right? And tons of people figure these were four of the disciples who followed Jesus around. But there was no one listed in the Bible named either Luke or Mark as a disciple. So these are more likely the names of people who are credited with passing on the legacy of these particular stories and/or perspectives to others.

We don't know for sure if any of those four guys actually followed Jesus around. And chances are really good that none of the people who finally wrote these down actually were disciples of Jesus. A good number of the disciples were probably illiterate anyway, so unless they were struck by some savant-like lightning bolt of literary skill, they couldn't have written them down. And chances also are that all the original disciples of Jesus were martyred for being Christians before these were believed to have been written anyway.

Most scholars believe the book of Mark came first: around 50 to 70 years after Jesus was born. Now, it would be nice to imagine Jesus lived that long, but he died when he was 33 (on account of the whole being crucified thing). So these stories were handed down for decades, and finally someone thought, "Man, we should just write this down so we won't lose them." Or maybe several someones. It was common back then in these cultures to put someone's name on something even if they didn't write it, just as it was common to steal writing from someone else and put your own name on it. If we did that now, we'd be in copyright court for years, sorting it all out. But back then, such practices were considered to be honoring of the person we attributed to or stole from (in the four Gospels in particular, this is called the "Synoptic Problem"[2])

So this is why I keep talking about biblical books by saying the letters "attributed to Paul," or the Gospel "attributed to," or "according to" Luke. Doesn't mean some dude named Luke ever put pen to paper. It just means someone named Luke was probably instrumental in passing those stories along.

So why start with Matthew if Mark actually was written first? This is all debatable, but consensus tends to be because Mark doesn't start with Jesus' birth. In fact, it jumps right in at the beginning of Jesus' ministry when he gets baptized by his cousin, John the Baptist (AKA, locust-eating weirdo). So those guys who were putting the Bible together a few centuries after Jesus' life (remember the Council of Nicea from the previous chapter) figured it made more sense to put Matthew first, given that it has a kick-ass birth story. But Matthew and Luke probably weren't written for another 20 to 40 years after Mark. So keep in mind that those authors would likely have had Mark to draw from when they wrote Luke and Matthew.

And some navel-gazing theologians believe there's actually some mysterious lost text they call "Q" that all three of those Gospels used to jump off from. But that's definitely another book and too much in the weeds for our purposes here.

Then there's John. If you've ever read the Gospels, you might notice the whole vibe of John is really different than the other three. In fact, the Council of Nicea argued a lot about whether or not even to include John in the Bible. First off, it was really different, starting with this kind of poetic, mystical hooba-joob that was anything but literal. Second, it was written a good deal later than the other three, coming more than a century after Jesus' birth. So like the Apocrypha, it was up to a vote. John made it; the apocrypha was kept separate, and later deemed heresy (i.e., icky) by Protestants.

So picture the four Gospels as taking four different approaches or perspectives to the same story. It's kind of like how

Barbara Kingsolver wrote *The Poisonwood Bible.* By getting four distinct perspectives, the hope is that the reader can get a richer understanding about the life, teaching and ministry of Jesus.

Now, I ask you: if the Bible was so stinkin' clear, why did we need four books to tell the same story?

Then we have what are called the epistles, which is just a fancy word for "letters." These were messages attributed to Paul (there's the word again: attributed) and were written to different "house churches" around the territory. Most of them were really underground but growing, but they also had infighting, crises and crap the same way Christians do today. Some of them freaked out and ran for the hills when they found out the Roman authorities had put a price on their heads. Some were discouraged that Jesus hadn't come back in physical form yet. Some of them probably argued about what color carpet to have in the sanctuary! No wait, that's today...

Some of the epistles were words of encouragement, while others were more instructive. A good number of the folks starting these churches knew very little about the cultures where they were now operating. So the epistles sometimes broke down the dos and don'ts of the people they were ministering to and with. But ultimately, he was trying to get them to hang in there, stick with it and not lose hope or totally fall apart. And then we come along today and assume every word of those letters can apply to us, as if Paul (or whoever actually wrote the letters) could ever have imagined the Church of today.

See why it starts to get weird?

There are other books attributed to other folks, but that's the majority of the New Testament. The big one lots of people wonder about is Revelation (note no "s") which is considered prophetic. Some people think prophecy means to tell the future. But generally, prophecy is meant to reveal something, whether it's meant to be taken literally or not. There are debates about whether the author (or authors) of Revelation were in their right mind, writing in code or something else. In fact, this was another book that almost didn't make the biblical cut, namely because it's so freaking weird.

So the Bible was written in three languages (or more if you count Aramaic as technically more than one) by who-knows-how-many people over centuries and from different cultures. And you can break the Bible down into a handful of categories:

- **Myth** - story not necessarily meant to be taken literally, but part of a culture's attempt to take on big questions and reveal wisdom or truth.
- **History** - meant to be more specific accounts of actual events, or at least how people remembered them or had

been told about them by others.

- **Poetry** - Psalms are the best example of this, though anywhere in other books of the Bible you see the words written in stanzas rather than reaching from one side of a column to the other, that's poetry, meant to be recited aloud, or even sung.
- **Gospels** - Think we covered that one.
- **Epistles** - Also covered unless you skipped it or dozed off.
- **Laws** - rules to help maintain social order in a particular culture. Some can be applied to any culture or time period (don't commit murder), while others were based on existing issues of sanitation at that time (kosher laws) or their understanding of how life and the world worked at the time (don't spill your seed...you know..."masturbate." Is it getting hot in here or is it just me?).
- **Prophecies** - as mentioned above, these are foretelling in some ways, but not meant to be a day-and-date future chronology like Nostradamus tried (and failed a lot) to do. Some of them were words of warnings, and some were based on dreams, visions or maybe some bad mushrooms they picked up at Woodstock.

Look at that! In just a few pages, you're a biblical scholar. Well, maybe not exactly, and I know this can be a little dry and tedious.

But it's important, even for non-Christians, to know. If you live in a culture - and we do - where pieces of the Bible are thrown at you out of nowhere or used on you as a weapon, it's helpful to know a little bit of background.

Now I pinky-promise, super-duper-pooper-scooper swear to stop making you wade through that stuff. Some might assume by now that the title of this chapter, "Bible Beat Down," was referring to what I just did to you. But that's just the set-up. Consider it your scholarly spinach before we grab some spoons and lay waste to some brownie bottom sundae.

The Bible Clearly States...

Lots of parts of the Bible are used to prove particular points or to claim some ultimate "Truth." But there are particular ones used pretty often to justify what seems to be less-than-Jesus-like toward others. We even have a way of using Jesus' own words sometimes to scare the hell out of people (literally). Too often, I've met folks who simply accept this is what the Bible—and even the whole of Christianity—is all about. Even those of us within the Christian community who don't agree with these interpretations often don't have a strong enough understanding of scripture to offer an alternate understanding of the texts. Instead, we try to pretend the hateful, fear- or judgment-based religion isn't really there, or we just shake our heads and try to distance ourselves from it.

That's where the, "I'm a Christian, but I'm not *that kind* of Christian" explanations come from. Okay, so we're not that kind of Christian, but what kind of Christian are we, if we're actually one at all? What do we make of these Bible passages that so many argue are abundantly clear in their claims? What defines us? What do we stand for, rather than what we're against, or what we're not? So let's look at some of these infamous texts to get a better handle on them.

First, we'll consider what often are called the "clobber passages." These are the scriptures used to judge, condemn and deny rights to those whose gender identity or sexual orientation aren't what we deem to be "normal." God created man and woman to be married, make a family and have kids, period. Simple, clean-cut and undebatable. But see, that's when Christianity often trips, falling face-first in a nasty puddle of it's own certainty. The history, cultures, theologies and values systems of those involved in creating the Bible are broad and very, very complex. And yet, we're sure, beyond any doubt, that *we know* what the authors (and therefore, God) meant. Case closed. "The Bible says it; I believe it. That settles it."

In the words of Samuel Jackson's character in *Pulp Fiction,* allow me to retort.

Here's a list of the so-called "clobber passages" from the front of the Bible to the back:

Genesis 2:24

Genesis 19

Leviticus 18:22 and 20:13

Romans 1:26-27

1 Corinthians 6:9

1 Timothy 1:10

Romans 1:31 and 2 Timothy 3:3

Jude 6-7

Consider a few general things about the culture and base of knowledge at the time these texts would have been written. For one, they didn't have the advantage of brain science, or biology and anthropology either. They had no idea tat sexual attraction and gender identity are, in many cases, born into us and coded in our brains. They had no studies to reveal to them that sexual activity between creatures of the same sex occurs within nearly every species on the planet. They didn't know some plants–and even a few animals–were inter-sex, or that others change sex during their lifetime. Things were more black-and-white; things like us were good, and everything else was bad.

But as the old saying goes, when we know better, it's on us to do better.

They also had an interesting idea about how procreation worked. Keep in mind that these tended to be highly patriarchal societies, in which men ruled and women not only weren't equals; they were actually treated as *property.* So in that spirit, it was deemed that, the man-juice led to life and came from the man, so obviously, men were the ones that *really mattered*.

Once again, though, we know better now. And yet, we aren't always so good at the *doing* better part. Anyway, with all of that in mind, let's go back to those clobber passages specifically used to condemn, LGBTQ people. We'll go from the top and work our way down...

Genesis 2:24 (Man cleaving to his wife)

> *Therefore shall a man leave his father and his mother, and shall cleave unto his wife: and they shall be one flesh.*

In Genesis Adam is saying this after Eve has been created. God removes one of his ribs and makes her, so we could say that Eve was "bone-worthy." But I digress...

So Adam has this new partner, and if they don't get busy making some babies, the entire human race is doomed. Oh, and they're completely naked and he's never been laid. So yeah, she seems inherently appealing to him. But here's a curiosity I raised that got me kicked out of youth group: if Adam and Eve were the first two people on the planet, who was he saying this to? And why the heck is he talking about leaving parents? There was no such thing yet.

While we're at it, at what age does it become a sin not to leave your parents and marry? Back in the time of Jesus, girls were married off (frequently to significantly older men) as soon as they had their first periods. So is God offended if we wait to leave home and get married until we're twenty-somethings? When does not leaving and cleaving become "abomination?"

But of course, we hone in on the interpretation that works for us, which is that "God intended" for man and woman to be together since Adam said it (metaphorically unless you're a literalist). Therefore homosexuality is against the will of the Creator. It takes a lot of reading into it to get there, but you can see the logic. The one sex organ is just meant to work in the one other sex organ and that's it. That's why this tends to be more of a backup clobber passage than the initial go-to text. It is, however, cited often in the fight against marriage equality for same-sex couples.

Genesis 19 (Sodom and Gomorrah)

It's pretty long, but worth reading. The story is about the cities of

Sodom and Gomorrah. And yes, this is where the modern word "sodomy" came from. It's quite the read, and not because there's tons of rampant gay sex happening. In fact, from early on it starts off with this guy named Lot handing over his really young virgin daughters to a pissed off crowd to be gang-raped in exchange for the mob not trashing his place and killing everyone. Nice, right? But you don't hear Christians using this to justify gang-raping preteen virgins. Which, hooray for that.

It's common for people to suggest that God destroyed Sodom and Gomorrah because everyone was kicking things up into orgiastic gay sex parties. But biblical scholars who studied the background of the city generally have a much better explanation of the "sodomy" going on in these cities. It's much more likely that this was part of a "pagan," i.e. non-Jewish religious practice, which the Jews would have seen as good reason for their God to be pissed off. Also, the great "sin" spoken of in the story of which these cities were guilty was that they treated the poor and outsiders badly, focusing only on themselves.

And like most all other biblical stories, this was written after the event. The cities had already been plundered by outside forces, so it was reasonable to ask why these great cities suddenly fell and why not make it a cautionary tale to keep law-abiding Jews on the righteous path?

Just out of curiosity, what do you suppose was in the water, exactly, that made two entire cities suddenly crave gay sex? Or if they did all really become gay (an anomaly for the ages, for sure), couldn't God have just waited a while until they all died out? A whole city full of gay people would have no babies. No progeny, no problem.

Leviticus 18:22

> *Thou shalt not lie with mankind, as with womankind: it is abomination.*

and 20:13

> *If a man also lie with mankind, as he lieth with a woman, both of them have committed an abomination: they shall surely be put to death; their blood shall be upon them.*

There are several things to understand about these passages, and all of it requires considering them in a larger context. First, if this was important to Jesus wouldn't he say something? Interestingly, most Christians who believe these verses *love* to quote from Paul, sometimes more than Jesus himself. But if we consider what Paul had to say about the original Jewish laws from the Torah, he's pretty clear. Here are a few examples:

All who rely on observing the law are under a curse... (Galatians 3:10)

But if you are led by the Spirit, you are not under law. (Galatians 5:18)

Effectively, he's saying if you're living your life according to the previous laws, you're not on the Jesus train. After all, Jesus' intent was to unbind us from the tyranny of the rule of law (or more specifically, how we use it against each other), rather than to continue to lean on it to oppress or condemn each other.

And yet, here we are.

Also, there are lots of explicit points throughout the Bible that state you can't pick and choose which of the laws you'll follow and which you don't:

For whoever keeps the whole Law and yet stumbles at just one point is guilty of breaking all of it. (James 2:10)

There are other examples in this same spirit throughout the book of Galatians and elsewhere saying roughly the same thing. The point as I see it is that we're all going to screw it up. Therefore the only way out of that cycle is to be freed from it. The point, it's argued by Jesus and echoed by Paul, is that we're hopelessly imperfect left to ourselves. And in the Christian story, the embodiment of perfect grace (freedom through forgiveness) is found in God, as revealed by Jesus.

Put another way: you're never going to be good enough on your own. So stop killing yourself trying to be, and beating yourself up when you fall short. And beyond that, stop beating others up because they're not meeting your interpretation of the law.

Another important piece to understand is that these two texts from Leviticus are a part of a much bigger chunk–Leviticus, chapters 17 through 26–that are known as the "Holiness Code." It's believed by Bible scholars to have been written separately from the rest of Leviticus, likely by priests, and inserted later into the book. The intent of this was to steer people away from sexual acts used as part of other religious rituals, including same-sex prostitution. It was pretty common for Jews to drift away from traditional Judaism and adopt some (or lots) of these "pagan" practices, many of which involved sexual--and sometimes same-sex acts, so this was a rulebook to tell you what not to do.

So sorry folks, but gay prostitution as a way of honoring God is out.

Romans 1:26-27 (Vile affections)

For this cause God gave them up unto vile affections: for even their women did change the natural use into that which is against nature: And likewise also the men, leaving the

natural use of the woman, burned in their lust one toward another; men with men working
that which is unseemly, and receiving in themselves that recompense of their error which was meet.

This is one of the letters attributed to Paul and written to those in the Christian community in Rome. It's always interesting to me when Paul is quoted to diminish or condemn gays or women (we'll get to that), because he also said in Galatians 3:28 that "There is neither Jew nor Greek, there is neither bond nor free, there is neither male nor female: for ye are all one in Christ Jesus." But then there's this stuff about "vile affections" and women keeping silent in church, covering their heads and so on. So which is it, Paul? Gah!!!

What's going on in this Romans text anyway? Keep in mind that Rome was rife with religious practices that incorporated animal sacrifice, orgies and the like, so Paul was equipping his brand new Christians with a sort of guide to what fell within the Christian culture and what didn't fly. After all, they were told by Paul to know the culture around them and integrate themselves into it. Yet, there were to be limits. In the "Journal of the Evangelical Theological Society," which is basically a clubhouse for Bible scholars, Catherine Kroeger said this about the religious practices common in Rome at that time of the Romans text:

> *Men wore veils and long hair as signs of their dedication to the god, while women used the unveiling and shorn hair to indicate their devotion. Men masqueraded as women, and in a rare vase painting from Corinth a woman is dressed in satyr pants equipped with the male organ. Thus she dances before Dionysos, a deity who had been raised as a girl and was himself called male-female and 'sham man.' ...the sex exchange that characterized the cults of such great goddesses as Cybele [Aphrodite, Ishtar, etc.] the Syrian goddess, and Artemis of Ephesus was more grisly. Males voluntarily castrated themselves and assumed women's garments. A relief from Rome shows a high priest of Cybele. The castrated priest wears veil, necklaces, earrings and feminine dress. He is considered to have exchanged his sexual identity and to have become a she-priest."*

So these religious prostitutes actually did the circuit throughout Rome performing these kinds of orgies, specifically within pagan temples. So this is what Paul knew, and it was what he would have been responding to in the letters to his Roman Christians. Pretty much: that stuff isn't cool. I have to agree with Paul on that one.

1 Corinthians 6:9 (All the no-nos)

> *Know ye not that the unrighteous shall not inherit the kingdom of God? Be not deceived: neither fornicators, nor idolaters, nor adulterers, nor effeminate, nor abusers of themselves with mankind.*

This text, along with all of Paul's writing, was in Greek, so we actually have to go back to the root language to understand what's up here. The word translated as "effeminate" in the King James Bible is μαλακός (malakós), and it appears in lots of other places in the New Testament, usually translated as "soft," but also as something else. This is the only place that word is translated as "effeminate," though, which is a little bit weird. So what did he actually mean? Hard to say, since there's no word in Greek that actually translates into anything like what some call "effeminate men" today. It could be referring to just this, or it could be about weakness of character, laziness or something else. To me what's most interesting is the choice of the King James translators to choose "effeminate" in this one and only place.

The next phrase, "abusers of themselves with mankind," comes from a word that is a mashup of two other words, "male" (ρσην) and "bed" (κοίτης). But this isn't a common Greek compound word. In fact, it doesn't show up anywhere else in scripture outside of Paul's writings. So where we translate it as "abusers of themselves with mankind," we only have "man-bed" as a root source.

So let that be a warning to all of you who see yourselves as man-beds; you've been officially put on notice!

1 Timothy 1:10 (The "Man-Bed")

> *For whoremongers, for them that defile themselves with mankind, for menstealers, for liars, for perjured persons, and if there be any other thing that is contrary to sound doctrine.*

First off, the word in question here actually isn't what you think. It might seem reasonable that "menstealers" could be referring to guys who take other women's men, but that's referring to slave brokers. It's actually "them that defile themselves with mankind," which sounds a lot like the phrase in Romans above, right? You'd be right if you thought so, because it's that same pesky invented compound word. Must have been a whole lot of man-beds back in the day.

A more recent translation, the English Standard Version, uses the word "homosexual," but that word not only didn't exist in Paul's time; it didn't even exist when the King James translation was done. Then there's the Jerusalem Bible, which translates this word as "those who are immoral with boys." Other translations use "perverts" or "sodomites."

So what's the answer? We're all trying to make educated guesses, but if the meaning were entirely crystal clear, we wouldn't have all of these variations.

Romans 1:31 (Without Natural Affection)

> *Without understanding, covenantbreakers, without natural affection, implacable, unmerciful...*

and 2 Timothy 3:3

> *Without natural affection, trucebreakers, false accusers, incontinent, fierce, despisers of those that are good...*

The key phrase here is "without natural affection," and we'll get to that in a minute. But these both are excerpts from larger lists of depraved sins of which Paul feels Christians are too often guilty. These lists include things like infighting, gossip, breaking promises and showing a lack of mercy toward others. But of course, we hone in on the abundantly clear phrase "without natural affection" instead. I mean, if I had a nickel for every time I accused someone of being without natural affection...well, I'd be pretty damn broke. But anyway...

So what does "without natural affection" mean? Not surprising that other Bible translations have slotted this, once again, into the "homosexuality" category. But pull up the original Geek and the root word is "sterego," which is one of four words used in Greek to mean "love." Unlike us, the Greeks have lots of different linguistic treatments of this elusive, complicated and loaded word. Instead, we throw "love" around for all kinds of things, and then wonder why there's so much confusion.

There is "eros," which refers to romantic love (the Barry white, bearskin rug kind). Then there's "philios," which is a sort of brotherly love, or camaraderie. That's why Philadelphia is the city of brotherly love. Third is "agape," which is a sort of spiritual love: the kind of love that should fill someone who embraces all equally, without exception. That's why you'll see churches named things like Agape Christian Church. It's a goal they're trying to strive for in their community.

"Sterego," though, is love that family members have for one another. So the word used in both of these verses is "asterego," and the "a" negates whatever comes after it, just like someone today who is amoral is without morals. So someone "without natural affection" is one who doesn't show natural familial love toward their spouse, children, parents or another family member. So an example of this might be, say, kicking your teenage daughter to the curb for getting pregnant, or maybe cutting off all ties with your son because he's gay.

So it's actually bitterly ironic when someone uses these to condemn homosexuality, as they're actually acting with a sort of "asterego" toward others.

I think it's also helpful, especially in the case of the Romans verse, to read a little further, to Romans chapter 2, verses 1-4:

> *Therefore, you may think you can condemn such people, but you are just as bad, and you have no excuse! When you say they are wicked and should be punished, you are condemning yourself, for you who judge others do these very same things. And we know that God, in his justice, will punish anyone who does such things. Since you judge others for doing these things, why do you think you can avoid God's judgment when you do the same things? Don't you see how wonderfully kind, tolerant, and patient God is with you? Does this mean nothing to you? Can't you see that his kindness is intended to turn you from your sin?*

Ah, but judging and condemning others is so fun! Definitely more enjoyable than dealing with my own mess. And I think that gets to the heart of the whole debate. Generally when we focus so intently on what we perceive to be the sins of others, it's because there's something we see in them that reminds us of ourselves. This isn't to say that every fire-breathing, Bible-thumping gay basher is secretly gay (though I'd bet good money that there's a higher incidence of repressed homosexuality among that demographic than in the rest of the population); but focusing on something that's so out in the open about their sexuality helps distract us from the powerful, complex and inescapable reality of staying on a path of sexual thinking and living that truly honors ourselves and others. It's hard, scary work that often carries so much shame and guilt with it that its power just grows when ignored. So we look outside of ourselves instead, taking out the conflict and internal judgment we're scared to wrestle with on others because it's easier to pick on them.

If anything in the world is far from Christ-like, it's that.

Jude 6-7 (Going after strange flesh)

> *And the angels which kept not their first estate, but left their own habitation, he hath reserved in everlasting chains under darkness unto the judgment of the great day. Even as Sodom and Gomorrha, and the cities about them in like manner, giving themselves over to fornication, and going after strange flesh, are set forth for an example, suffering the vengeance of eternal fire.*

We don't actually need to spend too much time on this one, mostly because it's super duper weird. The whole thing is about angels acting less than angelic. Basically they give up their heavenly duties to go have sex with human beings. So bad news for all you angel-fetish folks, but you're contributing to the delinquency of God's butlers. Knock it off, will ya?

It's common, though for those seeking anti-gay ammunition just to grab onto the phrase "going after strange flesh," and run with it. But if you want to talk about going after strange flesh, that sounds like the sin of eating hot dogs to me. There's no meat product - short of maybe SPAM or Vienna sausages - stranger than cylinders of animal leftovers shoved into the small intestine of some animal and served with ketchup. Gross.

So What?

If you're getting the sneaking sense that even some translators of scripture—or maybe even some of the original authors themselves—are at least operating from an undeniable subjective personal or cultural viewpoint, if not operating with an outright agenda, congratulations! You're becoming a critical engager of the Bible. And to approach scripture critically doesn't mean to dismiss it or write off those bits we wrestle with. Rather, we should strive to understand where they're coming from, what they wanted to communicate and why. And at best, we should still try and glean the wisdom or truth from their words, even when it's ultimately not what we believe today.

Finally, it's important to note that neither during Paul's time, nor when many of these modern translations were done, did people understand the immutable nature of sexual orientation and gender identity. We didn't have neuro-imaging or things like the Kinsey sexuality spectrum studies to help us have a more nuanced, sophisticated understanding of how human sexuality works. And we certainly have no references anywhere in scripture to people in a committed same-sex relationship. Even with all the different interpretations, the few mentions of anything resembling homosexuality boil down to particular sex *acts*. Many have to do with prostitution, sexual pagan rituals, pedophilia or military rape. None refer to *being gay*.

And as for Christians, we tend to look to Jesus for the final word on matters of dispute. So what does he say about homosexuality? Absolutely nothing. Not a word. What he does say is not no judge others, to focus on our own hearts and lives, to love all others without exception or condition. If we look to his example for what to do when dealing with populations who are often pushed to the margins, excluded or branded as immoral, the message seems pretty clear. We are to reach out, treat them as equals, include them, love and advocate for them.

When we know better, we do better. So let's get to work on doing better.

CLOBBER PASSAGES: THE BOARD GAME

Other parts you'll need:

- Game piece for each player
- One die

DIRECTIONS

- Put game pieces at START square
- Each player rolls the one die
- Move your game piece forward as the one die indicates
- Follow the directions in each square where you land.
- If you land on "PURGATORY," you have to stay there until someone else lands there and takes your place (through intercessory prayer, of course). They are then stuck until someone else frees them.
- First player to go all the way around the board three times (because of the Trinity) wins!

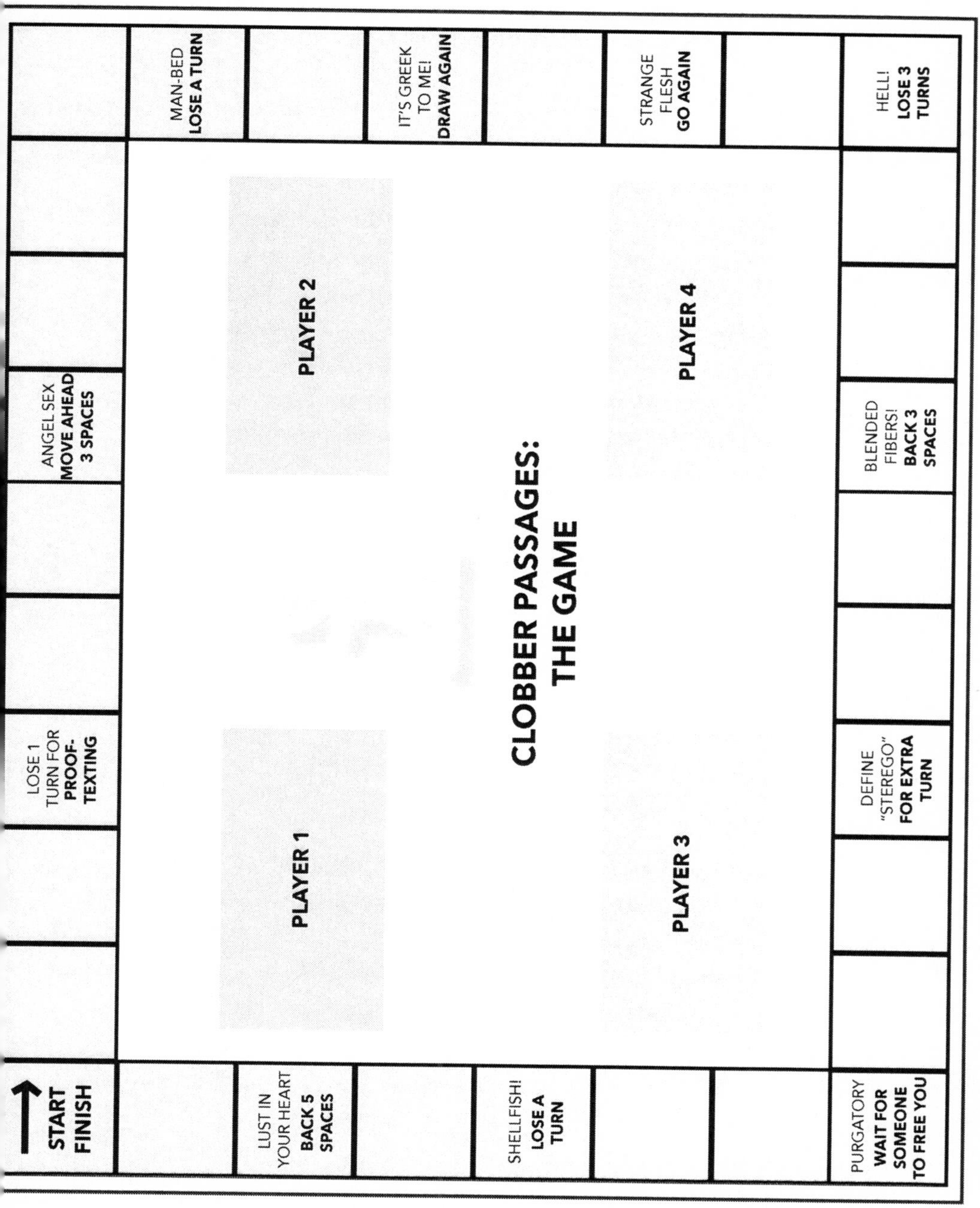

START
FINISH

LOSE 1 TURN FOR **PROOF-TEXTING**

ANGEL SEX **MOVE AHEAD 3 SPACES**

MAN-BED **LOSE A TURN**

LUST IN YOUR HEART **BACK 5 SPACES**

PLAYER 1

PLAYER 2

IT'S GREEK TO ME! **DRAW AGAIN**

SHELLFISH! **LOSE A TURN**

CLOBBER PASSAGES: THE GAME

STRANGE FLESH **GO AGAIN**

PLAYER 3

PLAYER 4

PURGATORY **WAIT FOR SOMEONE TO FREE YOU**

DEFINE "STEREGO" **FOR EXTRA TURN**

BLENDED FIBERS! **BACK 3 SPACES**

HELL! **LOSE 3 TURNS**

WHAT THE HELL?

When I was a kid, hell was a real place, and it was close. I mean like, "shake it once to many times in the bathroom and you might become a briquette" close. One time I was volunteering in a Sunday school class for kindergarteners and, of course, they were goofing off. The teacher turned to one of the boys who was particularly uninterested in what she had to say, leaning within inches of his little face.

"You think this is funny, don't you?" she scowled. "You like to make jokes instead of listening to the lesson, right? Well, what if this is the one time your heart is really open to Jesus and you're missing it? Or what if this is the only time in their lives your friends will ever hear about how Jesus died to save them from hell? What if, because of your messing around, your friends go to hell and burn forever? Are you ready for that responsibility? Do you think that's funny?"

Of course the boy was in shock and nearly in tears. Not surprising, the room was still and quiet as death the rest of the lesson. But it was then that I realized how important hell was to Christians, or at least the Christians I knew. It was a way to keep kids in line. It gave every sermon a sense of urgency, and the fact that the pastor was offering you the only key to the door out of that fiery eternity of despair, emptiness and basic cable made it an offer too good to refuse.

In short: it was the best recruiting and discipline tool ever invented.

I've known scads of people who accepted Jesus and became Christians for the sole purpose of ensuring they didn't end up going to hell. It's a lot like something that famous mathematician and philosopher Blaise Pascal once said, now known as "Pascal's Wager." In a nutshell, he said that there was a lot more to lose in not believing in God. So act as if God exists, and there's really no consequence. If you live like God doesn't exist and God really is there to condemn you, you've made the ultimate mistake.

Works out well for the ones who claim to hold the winning hand in that wager, right? It starts to explain why so many ministries are nearly obsessed with hell and all the bad stuff that might happen to us, even if it makes them seem pretty loony, even a herd of ranting assholes.

We can argue day and night about whether or not fear-based theology is effective, biblically accurate or even necessary. But it's worthwhile to consider where our contemporary ideas about hell and Satan come from, given that those are the sort of cornerstone icons for fear-driven Christian conversion and recruitment. A lot of folks assume it's just all in the Bible, plain as day, and generally, those who teach it will affirm that assumption. But the way we think and talk about hell and Satan today is a barely recognizable derivative of what's in Jewish and Christian scriptures. In fact, Jewish texts don't mention hell at all. It's just not a part of what they believe. Actually, we have pagan religion and popular culture to thank more than anything.

Thanks, Dante.

So with your indulgence, ahem, I'll go a little old-school evil on your ass. We'll start with Satan; save hell for dessert.

Please Allow Me to Introduce Myself...

Our understanding–and misunderstanding–of the devil starts all the way back in Genesis. Some understand the serpent in the Genesis story to be an incarnation of Satan. But Satan first emerges in the Old Testament by name in I Chronicles, and again in Job. His primary role is to demonstrate the weakness of humanity in the face of hardship.

In Job, Satan actually asks for permission from God to prove the fragility of Job's faith by submitting him to any number of hardships. Satan's feelings about people are summed up in Job 2:4, when he claims, "Skin for skin! All that people have they will give to save their lives."

He shows up again in similar form in II Samuel and Numbers, always as the antagonist. The name *Satan* actually means 'adversary.' While some may assume this means he is God's adversary, it's more accurate to think of him as humanity's adversary, always trying to show how unworthy we are of God's love.

In the Old Testament, Satan has no latitude to operate outside of what God gives him permission to do. Think of him more like a prosecuting attorney, beholden to God's judiciary authority. He actually works alongside God instead of against God. You could also think of him like a super-jealous big brother, trying to convince his dad that his faith in and love for the new baby is unfounded.

Some people also mistakenly refer to Satan as Lucifer. But the word "Lucifer" means "Light Bearer" in Latin, which was the term used to describe the planet Venus. Some people take Isaiah 14, about Lucifer's fall, to be a story about Satan being cast out from heaven, since it looks similar to a quote in Luke. However, most biblical scholars and historians say that this interpretation is taken out of context.

The "Morning Star" actually was a term commonly used to describe the Babylonian Empire. The king of Babylon not only oppressed the Israelites (God's chosen people in the Jewish scriptures), but he also made a habit of comparing himself to God in the scope of his power. With this understanding, the scripture in Isaiah actually is prophesying the fall of the Babylonian Empire.

As for the use of the names "Lucifer" and "Satan" interchangeably in the Bible, it doesn't happen. Satan is not described as Lucifer until secular literature like John Milton's *Paradise Lost* adopted them as pseudonyms. From there, the name seeped into our culture until we mistakenly began taking it as sacred scripture.

Satan is much more prevalent–and more powerful–in the New Testament. He possesses people, tempts Jesus, and Jesus even claims to see Satan in others, including Peter, his most faithful disciple.

Some maintain that Satan is an actual physical being, while others understand the stories about Satan more metaphorically, representing the constant weakness of the flesh. But regardless of how you see it, there is one thing most of us can agree on: evil exists.

Theologian Frederick Buechner says that evils exists because, in being allowed to choose whether or not to love God and one another, we also have the choice whether or not to live out our evilest impulses. In this way, Satan lingers in our choices rather than in the shadows, and in the mirror rather than the depths of hell.

Now, that's scary stuff.

Inventing Hell

While Jonathan Edwards wasn't the first to preach about hell and condemnation, his 'Sinners in the Hands of an Angry God' sermon in 1741 crystallizes the beginning of a modern movement in the church. Edwards employed fear of punishment as a primary means for conversion and doctrinal adherence. Meanwhile, his congregants fainted in the aisles and clung to the pews to avoid being dragged down into the abyss.

We can argue day and night about whether or not fear-based theology is effective, biblically accurate and even necessary. But it's worthwhile to consider where our contemporary ideas about hell even come from.

First, we have to consider what it is we're talking about when we say "hell." Is it a place of eternal conscious torment? Is it effectively the same as the annihilation of the soul, when one ceases to exist, even in the spiritual sense? Is it less physical and more of a conscious torment, where we, bound by our sins, spend eternity aware only of our irreconcilable separation from God?

Is it something awful but not eternal? Can we earn our way out? Does it have different levels like Dante's "Inferno?" For the sake of this discussion, I'm working under the assumption that the "hell" we're talking about is one of eternal conscious torment and suffering. Never mind if the suffering is physical or just psychic; eternal conscious suffering in itself is probably bad enough, either way.

Consider for a second that phrase, "eternal conscious suffering."

Eternal. By definition, eternity has no beginning or end. So if we're to be condemned there forever, are we already there? Now, some would argue that life on earth is hell enough, but even the most ardent Christian apologist would not suggest that this, here and now, is hell (I told someone at my church about having a two-hour debate on this topic and that sounded like hell to him).

Next, consider the word *conscious*. Consciousness is only made possible by the human brain, a tool that helps us know who, where and when we are. Without it, we have no awareness of the distinction between us, our inner world and the rest of the outer world. Without consciousness, there is no

"I" or "other." At the point of physical death, consciousness, i.e. cognitive function, stops.

Is there such a thing as "soul consciousness?" Perhaps. But how and for what purpose? To what end? In Romans 8 verses 38-39, the Apostle Paul tells us that "neither death, nor life, nor angels, nor rulers, nor things present, nor things to come, nor powers, nor height, nor depth, nor anything else in all creation, will be able to separate us from the love of God in Christ Jesus our Lord." Does that mean our consciousness goes on forever?

In first John, chapter 4, verse 8, we have one of the most famous verses in scripture: "Whoever does not love does not know God, because God is love." Note that it doesn't say "God is like love,' or "God has love." It says that "God" and "Love" are one and the same. So God is love, and nothing we can do in life or death can separate us from God.

Perfect unity with love, it seems, would eliminate the necessity for consciousness. The experience of oneness with God (which Paul says is inevitable because of Jesus) seems to mean the closing of the gap between "self" and "other." Unity. No separation, and therefore, no use for consciousness, never mind the scientific impossibility of human consciousness as we understand it continuing after physical death.

Third, we need to understand what it means to *suffer*. Suffering is different from pain. While pain is a physical thing involving nerves and the brain again, suffering is the emotional and/or psychological part. Though this can be brought on by physical pain, it can also be related to trauma, loss or separation.

And if such separation can and does exist beyond physical existence, we're left with a number of troubling questions we have to contend with, like:

- Why would a loving God condemn a soul to eternal suffering for a temporal decision based on false information acquired during their lifetime?
- Is God unable to look upon sin? If so, how did God create people with the capacity to do something he can't endure? Why then in the Book of Acts are even the disciples given the authority to forgive sin?

These questions present a conundrum, because if God *can't* expiate sin without our participation in asking for that forgiveness, then God can be seen as weak. If, instead, God *chooses not* to forgive sin unless we ask for it, opting instead to let us suffer for all eternity because of our mistakes, then God could be considered not loving.

In order to understand how the Bible presents the issue

of hell, we have to consider the many words often considered synonymous with "hell." In the Old Testament, the word "hell" appears 32 times. The phrase "the grave" is used 29 times, and "The pit" comes in at a distant third with three appearances. But all sixty-four instances of these words throughout the first 39 books of the Bible come from the same Hebrew Word, "Sheol."

In the Jewish tradition, *Sheol* is a resting place for the dead. While some believe this is the same as hell, there are indications to the contrary. In the ancient Jewish tradition, Sheol is a place of rest for both righteous and wicked, with no distinction.

Not all Jews were happy about this either.

In the third chapter of Malachi, the prophet recognizes the consternation of faithful Jews who are frustrated that the wicked share the same fate. In Ecclesiastes, the priest Koheleth claims that serving God is vanity. For him, the fact that the righteous are treated the same as the wicked and vice-versa should be a call to eat, drink and be merry.

With respect to any relationship between Satan in the Old Testament and *Sheol*, there is none.

In the New Testament, there are three words from the Greek that, when translated to English, are generally translated as "hell." One is Hades, which appears eleven times. Another is

Tartarus, which only shows up once. And the third is Gehenna, which comes up twelve times.

First, Hades. Approximately 3,500 years ago, the Greek practice of Hellenism emerged. Hellenism was practiced by the preponderance of Greek culture, valuing logic, knowledge, self-care and moderation. It was influential on Jewish culture, not only in the practices adhered to by the Greeks, but also with regard to their belief in the immortal soul and the afterlife that followed.

But despite its cultural influence on Judaism, and later, Christianity, it was considered to be a pagan, or gentile religion, and therefore not acceptable in the eyes of God.

Greek culture believed in a place called Hades, which was the resting place for disembodied souls. We see evidence of this in writing as far back as the 8th century B.C., in Homer's *Odyssey*. Hades is described as an Underworld, literally located underground; thus we can see the first indication of hell as subterranean.

Hades includes multiple levels, including Elysium and Tartarus. Elysium, also called Elysian Fields, can be equated with our modern idea of heaven. One difference–although Greek scholars did not always agree on where different levels of Hades were–is that we think of heaven as located above us, whereas the general consensus is that all levels of Hades were part of a larger *underworld*.

Tartarus was the level of Hades where unrighteous souls

dwelled. This correlates to our modern understanding of hell, where there is wailing, fire and gnashing of teeth as those who displease God pay an eternal price of their disloyalty. For the Jews of the time, this pagan Hellenistic belief was appealing because it helped justify their faithfulness. It gave reasons beyond any earthly consequence for following the laws of the Hebrew scripture.

How heavily did Greek culture influence Jewish tradition? Consider this: whereas the Old Testament was written in Hebrew, the original language of the New Testament is Greek. The influence of Greek culture can hardly be over-emphasized.

The writings of Flavius Josephus, a Jewish priest, had tremendous sway over early founders of the Christian church such as Origen, Justin Martyr and Irenaeus. Josephus, in turn, was particularly interested in Greek culture and ideology, as well as that of the Essenes, an ascetic Jewish network very focused on end-times theology and Jewish mysticism. Josephus' noncannonical texts such as *The Jewish War* and *Jewish Antiquities* were available to these church fathers, as well as to those who wrote the Gospel texts and other New Testament scripture, which is the source of our contemporary understanding of hell.

Finally, we'll take a quick look at Gehenna, which is actually Greek for two Hebrew words, "Gee" and "Hinnom." Translated literally into English, Gehenna means "The Valley of Hinnom."

This valley was notorious among the Jews, as it was the place where apostate Jews, worshipping the pagan god Baal and the Canannite God, Moloch, would go to conduct sacrifices. Here, they would burn their offerings to Baal, which included birds, sheep, and in some cases, even their own children.

Because of this, Gehenna was considered to be eternally cursed. It was also the site where Jerusalem's trash was taken to be burned. The site was considered so evil and repugnant that Jewish folklore told of a mythical gate in the valley which led directly down to a lake of fire.

Interestingly (and be forewarned this is a little graphic) when it rained, the ashes from the valley would be washed down to a nearby lake, at which point the fatty, animal-based remains would rise to the top of the water. If it came in contact with fire, the result would be that of a literal lake of fire, much like a burning oil slick on the surface of the ocean.

On the one hand, some Christians suggest we should play it safe and assume there is an actual hell, lest we lead people to the false assumption there isn't one, only to find out later we were wrong.

But considering the use of the doctrine of hell in the Christian faith, particularly in the past few centuries, suffice it to say that the fear, judgment, emotional scarring, family estrangement, physical violence and any number of holy wars that have been conducted in the supposed name of saving souls from such a place, we've created our own hell on earth.

Does hell exist? Perhaps. But the God of my understanding—the God revealed to me by the life and teachings of Jesus—is a God that seduces us, beckons us toward love, toward light. It is not a kingdom governed by fear and the avoidance of pain, but rather a kingdom in which the hungry are feed, the weak are empowered, and the desperate find hope.

Life has to be about more than buying the right fire insurance. 1 John 4:18 reminds us that there is no fear in love, and that perfect love drives out fear. We can be governed by one or the other, but we can't cling to both. I suggest love.

Purgatory: The Great Compromise

Dante's *Purgatory,* the second book from his *Divine Comedy,* is probably the best-known description of purgatory in popular literature. But it's definitely not the only one to talk about it. Shakespeare evoked images of purgatory in Hamlet, and the creators of the TV show, *Lost,* despite their assurance that the island was not in fact purgatory, referred to it thematically a lot.

Dante's trilogy follows the author through a first-person experience of hell, purgatory and then on to paradise. In his book, purgatory is a great mountain, located deep within the southern hemisphere. Virgil, Dante's guide, leads him through the seven levels of purgatory, each of which corresponds to one of the seven deadly sins. At the summit of the mountain is paradise, which is depicted as a return to Eden, the innocence of Adam and Eve, and a full reconciliation with God.

Although purgatory never is mentioned explicitly in the Bible, there are quite a few biblical bases used historically to argue purgatory's existence, both in the Old Testament (Dan. 12:10; Zech. 13:9; Mal. 3:2-3) and the New Testament (Mt. 5:21-26; Lk. 12:47-48, 12:54-59; I Cor. 3:12-15).

By now, you might be thinking: Why do some people believe such a place exists, especially if it is not specifically documented in scripture? On the other hand, what is the basis for the division between Catholics, the major proponents of the existence of purgatory, and Protestants who pretty much reject the idea? The answers to questions like this hold important clues about our wide-ranging understanding of sin, justice and mercy within the greater Church.

Many early scholars and God nerds talked about the idea of purgatory as early as the early third century, A.D. From Clement of Alexandria and Tertullian to St. Augustine two centuries later, and many others.[4] The idea of a holding place where humanity is held accountable for earthly screw-ups was around long before the term "purgatory" was used. In fact, it wasn't until a lot later that the Catholic Church even recognized purgatory as part of their official church doctrine.

It wasn't until Pope Gregory I that church leaders took an official stand on purgatory. In 1254, the Catholic Church adopted the concept as a part of their teaching. Gregory, who was a fanboy of St. Augustine of Hippo, took writing by Augustine produced about the possibility of a place like purgatory and used to make it an official part of church law.

In *The Story of Christianity,* Justo Gonzalez talks about the influence Augustine had on Gregory as Pope, seven centuries after his own death:

> *"What for Augustine was conjecture, in Gregory became certainty. Thus, for instance, the theologian of Hippo had suggested the possibility that there was a place of purification for those who died in sin, where they would spend some time before going to heaven. On the basis of these speculations of Augustine, Gregory affirmed the existence of such a place, and thus gave impetus to the development of the doctrine of purgatory.*[4]

In the sixteenth century, the Council of Trent – the people who made the rules for the Roman Catholic Church at the time

- affirmed the place of purgatory in church teaching. Oine reason they seemed to like it is because Protestants didn't, so it distinguished them further from one another. This further defined the differences in their understanding of salvation, which was super important to Martin Luther.

The idea of purgatory is that it prepares souls for the pure state in which they have to be in to get into heaven. One thing some theologians like about Purgatory is it helps them reconcile the idea of a God that is both a God of mercy and, at the same time, a God of justice (like the human kind of justice)[5]. It also offers a sort of incentive plan for staying active in church hand prayer life all of a person's life.

This way, the church didn't have to put conditions on God's grace - save for the cases in which an individual rejects God outright - so all who claim the faith are worthy of forgiveness. So how can this notion of grace for all be taught to the church's faithful, while also providing incentive for moral behavior? Purgatory fills this vacuum perfectly.

Literary scholar David Harris Sacks, in looking at purgatory imagery in *Hamlet,* recognizes not only the balance of justice and mercy in Shakespeare's piece, but also a healing and more peaceful call to action for the loved ones of the person who died:

"Purgatory, which provides the foundation for the medieval

forms, focuses on the cure of souls in the other world of the dead, where the justice of God is tempered with His mercy. It draws attention to what the living might do for the well being of those who have passed from this world, not to how they might avenge in this world wrongs experienced by the departed while still alive[6]."

In a medieval culture still plagued by bloody values of vengeance, purgatory calls the Christian faithful to prayer, rather than calling them to the sword. In this sense, purgatory for the friends and loved ones of a family member not only to remain connected to those we have lost, but also feel as like they have some way to help the person who died and advocate for their well-being. This offers an opportunity for healing in moments otherwise consumed by anguish and powerlessness.

In the Catholic tradition, contrition is only one step toward forgiveness of sins. A good Catholic also should make good for their transgressions. Generally, a priest determines penance, but at the time of death, a person (not a saint; they're all good) have to spend time in purgatory in order to purify themselves of the remaining sins carried over by their souls into the afterlife. Think of it like the final payoff on a loan you've made installment payments on but that has a remaining balance.

This period of temporary punishment can also be accelerated by the prayers for the dead performed by loved ones still living, as well as indulgences offered by the Catholic Church. Periods of time and degrees of severity of the punishment in purgatory are determined by the number and severity of unforgiven sins borne by the person when they die.

There are two types of sin: venial sins and mortal sins. Venial sins are not as bad an offense as the second kind. The sinner can reconcile themselves with God both by asking for forgiveness, and also by performing sacraments as dictated by a priest, or by taking part in holy communion.

Mortal sins are more severe, and by definition they sever the connection between God and the offender. These sins involve acts such as adultery, lying, murder, and can include things like skipping Sunday mass out of spite, or even using contraceptives (I'm screwed, pun intended). To be considered a mortal sin, the act in question has to have been done consciously, willfully, and with full understanding of the severity and consequences for doing it. In some cases, these types of sins can be forgiven, but given the varying badness of mortal sins, sometimes there may be justification for the sinner to be excommunicated, or kicked out of the faith forever.

The one unforgivable sin, even in purgatory, is said to be blasphemy (Mt. 12: 31-32), or willful rejection of the Spirit of God. This is the only one with no do-overs. For all other sins, there are varying degrees of severity determined by the church for each offense, and so time in purgatory, combined with earthly intercessory prayers (praying on behalf of someone else) and indulgences from the church, make right the soul who has enter heaven in a pure state.

Although lots of people in the Protestant tradition believe that salvation is limited only to those claiming Christ as their personal savior, the general sense of the Catholic Church is that it is available to the righteous of all faiths, provided that they reconcile themselves to the teachings of the church after death. Purgatory allows for this time of reconciliation to take place for pagans (the word for everyone else) and Christians alike. However, such an offense as not living one's life as a Christian may have more severe penalties, resulting in a longer sentence in purgatory.

This, of course, was an issue of great concern for those followers of Martin Luther who believed and taught that grace was achieved only through faith in Christ[7]. The notion that salvation was not limited to those claiming Christ was abominable. Further, early Protestants rejected the idea that indulgences and prayers could intercede on the behalf of the dead. In fact, prayers for the dead were specifically prohibited in the early Protestant movement[8].

Catholics holding fast to the existence of purgatory criticize the Protestant rejection of it as placing a limitation on God's grace. Protestants, on the other hand, think that the idea of paying for sins after you're already dead is a misinterpretation of the scriptural argument for salvation by faith. Catholics counter that if salvation were limited to God's elect who claim Christ, it would compromise His atonement, suffering and death. Basically, we love to argue a lot about stuff we'll never know for sure while we're alive.

In Jerry Walls' article, *Purgatory for Everyone*, he points out that the explicit presence or absence of biblical documentation does not seem to settle any debates about purgatory's existence:

> *"The fact that purgatory is not expressly present in Scripture is not enough to settle the issue, however. The deeper issue is whether it is a reasonable inference from important truths that are clearly found there. If theology involves a degree of disciplined speculation and logical inference, then the doctrine of purgatory cannot simply be dismissed on the grounds that Scripture does not explicitly articulate it[9]."*

It might seem like a pretty minor difference in interpretation to lots of us. But to take this big insider-baseball tangle and boil it down, the argument end up largely being about whether reconciliation can take place after death, and not whether being made right in the eyes of God is needed at all.

Other religions and sub-groups have beliefs that are sort of like purgatory, including Buddhism, Judaism and other orthodox Christian faiths. It's not just a Catholic thing, at least in concept. Regardless of our faith experience, we all tend to want to strike some logical balance between universal justice and mercy, so we can find a space in our faith practices for ourselves and others to seek righteousness while still having some greater accountability. But in the end, our opinions and theories about purgatory are a lot less important than the way we live out our understanding of God's mercy, love and justice from day to day.

In his book, *Wishful Thinking: A Seeker's ABC,* Frederick Buechner looks at the viewpoint of Catholicism from a Protestant perspective:

> *"What is persuasive about the Catholic view is the implication that even with God on their side people do not attain to what Saint Paul calls 'mature manhood, the measure of the stature of the fullness of Christ' (Eph. 4:13) overnight. At best the job is unlikely to be more than the slimmest fraction done by the time they die...Whichever side of the grave you are talking about, life with God apparently involves growth and growing pains...(but) many*

a high adventure awaits you and many a cobbled street before you reach the fountain in the square[10]*."*

Buechner celebrates a dynamic, rather than static, relationship with God. A Christian life is one based upon personal transformation and growth, only part of which can be achieved in a single lifetime in our ongoing efforts to become more Christ-like. Although we can't possibly know in its entirety what happens after we die, we all look forward together into the unknown with hope and anticipation. This, in turn, enriches our lives now, in the present, which he says is the point when we're interwoven as threads into the fabric of eternity.

Dude had a way with words.

So we celebrate God's paradise in the present, as a reality of our earthly experiences today, built upon the foundation of hope. This hope helps our lives be enriched and, when they pretty much suck, at least a little bit more tolerable because we have a sense that sometime, some way or another, there is something better waiting.

Ok, enough scholarly navel-gazing. Lets get back to regular English.

To Hell or Not To Hell?

Just because the Bible is interpreted lots of ways about something, or even doesn't say anything at all, doesn't mean it doesn't exist. It mentions nothing about abortion, gay marriage or the Internet either. Like Pascal's Wager, maybe it's better to assume hell is real than to believe it isn't and be wrong. I've heard this argument many times, especially when I've spoken against a theology centered on hell as a place of eternal torment. Hell, I even used it in trying to convert some of my Jewish classmates back in grade school (sorry guys).

There are times when I really hope hell is real, like when I hear about the enslavement of child soldiers. Grace just doesn't seem right for someone who can act with such disdain toward other people, especially kids. Then again, it's probably best for all of us that the universe doesn't hinge on my or anyone else's sense of what's right and fair.

My issue is primarily with whether someone believes there's a hell or not. The bigger issue is when we use it to scare or threaten people into believing or behaving the way we want them to. Not only is it questionable to use hell as a coercion tool; there's also an underlying arrogance in suggesting we know the criteria for going there—and they're usually pretty sure you're going and they're not.

Wouldn't it be bitterly ironic if, in the end, the only people who went to hell were those who believed in it and used it to scare the shit out people? That'd be the way it worked in my universe.

But I don't want that, really. OK, maybe a little bitty part of me–the five-year-old me–wants it, but that's as bad as those I'm hating. We all have it in us if we're being honest, so the trick can't be being perfect. We just need to recognize everyone needs grace and is entitled to it, and work a little harder at showing it to others–and the five-year-olds in each of us.

As for Christian logic, if the primary reason you want me to go to your church is because hell, by comparison, is at least slightly worse, you should probably work on your mission statement a little more before putting any more energy into evangelism. Being a follower of Jesus should be about a lot more than avoiding bad stuff; it's about making your life - here and now - better. Not necessarily easier, more comfortable or better by the typical earthly standards of success and happiness, but filled with more purpose, meaning and hope.

Plus, if it helps us be less asshole-ish to each other, isn't it worth at least thinking about it?fg

"WHERE THE HELL" WORD SEARCH

Test your damnation skills with this hellaciously hard puzzle!

```
R H P C T N U H Q P O N D Y C N Z A O R F A C F E
S U K J O K E D H U P J K A X Q Y Z O E W Z B D Z
L L H M T L V V T O V Q R Q R D G I I F K Y E I W
D W E P L Q K E T V N N K H G K Z B F I V L D Q Y
M D K F L F R G A N N E H E G O N M G C W V K S M
H O I R Q U E D E G W U N Z T K F E G U C F D L V
O R D W F B S L I T Q P K P B L M S S L Z R J B D
E K G H Z K X R O T S F C D I R H F X S A G G K D
N A X Q F G L O U V T I G L C N P I L W N S N V S
B Y M L F N W W B T O R M E N T F B D B W H F L W
N D Z S E Z J R Z I S Q G Z W E X E K W T A O G Y
D A N T E T C E P I O G V A O T B D R B X D W G G
Z D T J L X T D I L N O E H B O E M Y N U E Y A Y
Y E J A I H J N T I J I C J L K D S F Y O S E P T
A I O N S D R U R F L A F G U T Y J M W O N E T U
F F N O V U N E O K R H D B U T R A T A R U S C W
X H A N U R F R P Z X V B N I S K N L X Z Q W M X
L A T K E F Q N D Q S E M S B S R B O S G Y H T R
D R H B U V Z L X Z U H R V W G V S F M P G F X L
R L A S P S E K L T M N E B G E X U Q M W M B G X
O P N L I S W N P P P Q L L P S Q P N W T L D G G
R Z G X D O U W X Q V H I I L P M W C Y H I R Y A
W A W Y J V L C J U Z O T D I D B B Q J E V Z M V
O Q D E R U J Z C H X L O E H S I Q K V E E J R W
W I T P S S C M W B U N O W C Q I N U C T D F Y C
```

FIND THE FOLLOWING

1. Dante
2. Demon
3. Devil
4. Gehenna
5. Hades
6. Hell
7. Hellfire
8. Inferno
9. Jonathan Edwards
10. Lucifer
11. Outer Darkness
12. Satan
13. Sheol
14. Sin
15. Suffering
16. Sulphur
17. Tartarus
18. The Pit
19. Torment
20. Underworld

AN A** IS AS AN A**HOLE DOES

When I was in Kindergarten, I got into a fight with some of the kids in my neighborhood. They kept telling me that Santa Claus wasn't real and, of course, I insisted they were full of crap. It got heated and even a little bit physical–as physical as a six-year-old fight can get, anyway–until I ran home to my family. Everyone was there to celebrate Christmas: aunts, uncles and grandparents all enjoying the warmth of the fireplace and one of only six or so traditional Christmas carols that dominate the airwaves throughout December.

"Go...tell...them...Santa...is...real!" I managed between tearful sobs. My red face burned, both from the cold and the overwhelming emotion. The adults all stopped talking, stared at me, and then at each other and back to me again. It was the kind of look you get when someone has a hangy peeking out of their nostril, and no one wanted to be the one to say it.

"Well?" My voice reached a more frustrated pitch. "Go tell them!" More awkward silence. Finally my aunt pulled me up in her lap and, she began crying with me and broke the horrible, heartbreaking news. By the time she was done, everyone looked like they'd just witnessed an epic puppy-stomping. As my emotions began to level out, my brain kicked into gear and I turned around to look Aunt Sandra in the eye.

"But if Santa's not a real person," I said, "what about the Easter Bunny? What about the Tooth Fairy?" It was then that I realized that adults sucked. They lied to you for their amusement, just to join in with your friends and laugh at you for being so gullible. Kind of like when an older girl told me they took the word "gullible" out of the dictionary, then pointed and cackled when I believed her. At seven years old, I had no idea what the word meant anyway. But whatever, older people, as a group, were sadistic liars, bent on tricking impressionable children with stories they came up with just to laugh at us.

Sandra, the only honest adult in the universe, had laid it all out. She tried to explain about tradition, symbolism and how Santa represented something even bigger called the "spirit of Christmas." And it didn't help. But once I got past the initial shock and I was assured I still got to have presents, that word "spirit" stuck in my head.

What about God? What about Jesus? What about the hundred or so other people they had told me were real at church, like the snake that talked, the guy who got barfed up by a giant fish, or the miracles all over the New Testament? Frankly, they weren't any easier to believe than a fat guy who shoved himself down your chimney in the middle of the night to eat your cookies, stuff your socks and bring the good little children presents.

Come to think of it, Santa sounds creepy as shit.

My mom and aunt assured me that, without question, God and Jesus were real. But I wanted proof. After all, fool me once.... I wasn't falling for their spiritual Ponzi scheme again, though. We spent what seemed like hours (more likely ten minutes in Kindergarten time) talking about what was real and what wasn't, things seen and unseen and the like. And of course my dad, who was not the churchgoing type, kept his mouth tactfully closed. I wasn't sure what to believe, but I took them at their word, at least for the time being. Thus began my existential quest to de-santa-claus my life, culling through the lies to get down to what was really, really real.

Only later in school did I start to consider the differences between factual stories and myth or metaphor, and yes such words not only weren't uttered at church; to suggest something in scripture was myth, pointing to a bigger message, was blasphemy. You know how the rest of that story played out by now, but I remember that as the beginning of the end of my unconditional acceptance of anything that was told to me, simply because someone was old or could say it with a straight face. I was on my way to becoming a skeptic.

Thanks a lot, Santa.

Doing It For the Children?

Over the last two decades or so of working on and off within organized religion, one of the most common reasons I've heard young adults give for coming back to church—on the rare occasions when they still do at least—is to expose their kids to some kind of faith. For some, it's because they had a positive experience growing up in church; for others, it was some reason they struggled to put into words. They just feel like they should. Maybe they want them at least to know what a community of faith is about. Or to be exposed to "faith-based values." And there are those, despite the de-stigmatization of not going to church, that feel they'd be bad parents if they never let their kids learn the biblical stories they knew growing up.

But is religion really good for kids? Or are we doing more harm than good?

The answer, like lots of things, is complicated. And it probably depends on what kind of religious lessons they're exposed to. It's also relative to what you consider "good" religious lessons. Most studies have shown that kids who go to church on at least a fairly regular basis do exhibit more self-control and respond better to discipline, which is important to some parents. For those who want a more free-spirited kid, that may sound negative. There is some evidence, though, that religious training creates a small but measurable increase in a child's overall mental health. Of course, what that means is hard to define and some of that is reported by the parents themselves, who may be biased. But the trend is consistent and shows there are clear improvements in behavior and an overall sense of self for kids who go to church.

Whether it's church participation that actually causes the improvements, or whether it's other familial or cultural factors is unclear. It's the whole "correlation without causation" question. I spend quite a bit of time at coffee shops and I'm also a published author. And I bet if we did a study among all the authors in the world, we might find that they spend more time in coffee shops than average. But does that mean coffee shops are the secret? It's more likely because we have more opportunity and incentive to join the stereotype of the beard-stroking, latte-sipping writer.

I guess it's better than stroking lattes and sipping beards. Anyway...

There are some caveats to this argument that, at worst, religion has no effect, and at best, it's a net-positive. There's an argument in the psychology community that if there is significant disagreement or argument in the home about religion, this can create mental stress for kids. As one who grew up in a house where one parent went to church and the other didn't, I can say I always felt like I was letting someone down. Both of my folks worked, so time together on the weekend was a special but limited commodity. I wanted to be with both of them, and inevitably I felt guilty about whomever I wasn't with.

Did I mention I was one hell of a codependent little guy?

In fairness, though, my dad (the non-churchgoing one) rarely said anything negative about church, despite not being involved. He participated in prayers at meals and stuff, but hung out on the couch reading the paper and smoking cigarettes while I was in Sunday school. It was all good, more or less, until I got to my older teenage years when I began to question the things I was being taught at church. At the same time, they were having their own relationship issues, so my mom turned increasingly to her "church family" for support and connection. This, in turn, put even more distance between them, which my dad resented, and the cycle went in a downward spiral from there.

Divorces always have more going on under the surface

than most people realize, but one of the recurring themes I heard after they split was that their differences about religion were a significant factor in their final decision. So it's easy enough to see why I blamed religion—and sometimes even God—for breaking up my family.

There are findings, too, that kids who attend church and are exposed to Bible stories with miracles in them tend to have a harder time distinguishing between what's real and what's fantasy, magic and the like, in reality. They may also struggle to understand more legitimate cause-and-effect relationships in early life. So they may be more prone to believe that their dog died because they stole or that, say, New Orleans residents suffered from the broken levees because they disobeyed God. They can be more likely to attribute good things to God's blessing too, which can lean later in life to things like prosperity gospel teaching, or to blaming sin (theirs or that of others) for tragedies. This can compromise relationships, especially with those who don't see the world the same way.

Generally, though, the difficulties some religious children have separating reality, from fiction grow in their ability as they age, and some scientists argue that the effects of religious teaching on this aren't actually significant.

The biggest problems tend to arise around the messages

imparted to our kids about who they are, what they do or think, and their overall worth. For example, if a kid is gay and they hear over and over about the evils of homosexuality, it's easy to see how that could be damaging to their psyche. In fact, depression, anxiety and suicide are higher in general among gay kids, but even more so when they come from a religious background. And for heterosexuals, religion can lead them to be more judgmental or condemning.

A recent study in a biology journal looked at children ages 5 to 12 from Christian, Muslim and non-religious backgrounds, measuring their altruism and their degree of judgment of other child peers. They sampled nearly 1,200 kids from the U.S., Canada, China, South Africa, Jordan and Turkey and had them play a game called the "Dictator Test." Amazingly, a child by the last name of "Trump" scored the highest out of any of them.

Just kidding. But you know his grandkids might kick ass at the dictator game. God knows I'd never play "Risk" with the guy. Where was I?

Each kid was given a certain number of stickers, and was told there weren't enough to share with their group. They were asked to pay attention to the behavior of their peers, and the scientists assessed the perception of the parents of how their kids compared to others.

The conclusions were sobering. Regardless of religion or nationality, the religious parents reported they believed their children were more sensitive and empathic than kids of non-religious parents. Yet the exact opposite was true. The religious kids not only showed fewer altruistic tendencies, they were more readily inclined to use punishing behavior on their peers.

Though the parents thought their religious upbringing made their kids better, it may actually be that they were raising sanctimonious little assholes.

And for years, I was one of them. If my friends didn't come to youth group when I invited them, I waxed judgmental on them. And sometimes I focused far more on being right than being a good friend. On the one hand, I was praised at church for bringing more people into the proverbial fold than anyone else. On the other, I probably did just as much, if not more, to give myself and my faith a bad name to others.

Even worse, because we parents want to believe that putting kids in a religious environment helps make them better people, we see what we want to see. So does this mean church does more harm than good? Not necessarily. It depends in part on what sort of a religious environment they're exposed to. And unfortunately, although the "Little Dictator" study was pretty comprehensive in crossing boundaries of religion and nationality, there was no distinction made depending on the kind of teaching that was offered in each of those environments. So there's no real way of knowing if, like the obedience and behavior studies mentioned up top, kids are less prone to peer smackdowns and more inclined to be loving and compassionate if the mentors–and/or the God–they engage is more compassionate and less prone to jump to punitive measures.

Note to self: repeat study in spare time to fill in gaps scientists missed.

Maybe it just takes longer for the positive effects to show up? Maybe once they're of an age to make their own ethical choices, church kids show some positive distinction from their atheist friends?

Not so much, says a study done not long ago by Baylor University (yeah, *that* Baylor). These researchers found a direct relationship between a college student's degree of narcissism (how much they thought about themselves) and poor ethical behavior. And it didn't get any better whether the young adults were devoutly religious, only casually churchy or didn't go to church and didn't believe in God at all. And not only did being part of a faith tribe not improve ethical decisions; they still believed the same distorted things about themselves their parents apparently did. In short, even when they had internalized these stricter faith-based moral codes, and often believed they were living by them (even more than their atheist peers) they weren't.

Remember a while back when I mentioned that the two most common words Amy and I found were associated with Christians were "judgmental" and "hypocrites?" Those perceptions have been validated by empirical scientific study.

And it doesn't get any better when we get older, unfortunately. Back in 2012, another study (*Damn you, facts and science!*) asked a big group of Christians how many of them gave at least one-tenth of their income to charity, including their own church (ten percent being the common Christian teaching of "tithing").

One out of four Christians said they tithed, or even gave more than ten percent. But when participants actually let scientists compare their giving against their total income, only three percent gave even half that much. The study proposed that we've been taught to believe giving is the right thing, and we feel bad about not doing it, but the guilt is "comfortable guilt." We feel bad, but not bad enough to change. Not bad enough to tell the truth either. And maybe some of us have even gotten so used to the lie that we actually *believe it*.

So if we wonder why religious kids are assholes, and why we can't seem to see it, I wonder if it isn't because we're not *modeling* the better way. Instead, many Christian parents are praising and affirming how their kids are already acting morally superior because most of us want to believe that taking them to church makes them—and us—better people. But overall, it doesn't seem to.

And moreover, the world around us knows it. They see the lie we're telling them and ourselves too about how our way is the "right" way, and that our very living examples should be evidence enough of that. Meanwhile, all they see are a lot of self-deceived hypocrites, who would rather believe they're better people than do the hard work of making real, lasting change.

Now I'm showing why I peppered this book with jokes and amusing little games. If you're a Christian, this stuff is inescapably depressing. We're assholes, no doubt. And as my friend and fellow writer Peter Rollins says, if you're going to be a religious asshole, at least be honest about it. Well, he didn't say it exactly like that, but that's the general idea.

The hardest part, for me at least, is to see people outside of the church blaming God or Jesus for this ridiculous behavior. The whole "guilt by association" thing makes sense on the surface. And as I said, I've done it myself. But you don't sue the writer of the science textbook when the kid fails a test, especially if the kid didn't even study the book in the first place.

This takes us back to the beginning and why I loved my friend's sermon confession. We're Christians *because* we're assholes. And being a Christian doesn't help. In fact, it often ends up being worse when we become a complicit part of a system that tells us we're better people for being involved, and yet the evidence doesn't support it. So we're still assholes; now we're just hypocritical, deluded ones. And we judge those beyond the proverbial walls, partly because we can always see the faults in others more readily than our own, but also if we can convince them they're worse off than we are and they need to join us, it helps us validate ourselves: we're actually doing the right thing. Plus, it gets them to buy into the same illusion so they'll stop calling us on our hypocrisy.

We need to stop pretending and start doing the hard work of changing. It can seem like a thankless task, but it's vital if we're ever going to move forward. And the first thing we have to do is be clear about where we are. We owe at least that much to ourselves and our kids.

We can do better, even if we're all imperfect, selfish little assholes at heart.

JESUS MAD-LIBS

You played Mad-Libs when you were a kid, but probably not like this. Find a gullible friend (or maybe a kid) and ask them for the words required to fill in the blanks according to the types of words asked for in the parentheses.

Long ago, in a little ____(NOUN)____ called ____(PLACE)____, a child named ____(NAME)____ was born to Mary, a ____(NOUN)____ engaged to be married to____(NAME)___, a ____(OCCUPATION)____ from a land called ____(PLACE)____. One night, an angel ____(PAST-TENSE VERB)____ them and said they were to name the child ____(NAME)____. When the king heard about the child being ____(PAST-TENSE VERB)____, he ordered his ____(PLURAL NOUN)____ to ____(VERB)____ the child. But the new family escaped to ____(PLACE)____ just in time. As the child _(PAST-TENSE VERB)____ older, he brought to his ____(PLURAL NOUN)____ a simple and beautiful message: ____(VERB)____ others as you would like to be ____(PAST-TENSE VERB)____. People thought his ____(NOUN)____ was ____(ADJECTIVE)____ but they were ____(ADJECTIVE)____, so they ____(PAST-TENSE VERB)____. It's hard to ____(VERB)____, but apparently ____(PLURAL NOUN)____ have a hard time not being ____(PLURAL NOUN)__.

ONCE AN A**HOLE...

I'm not sure, but I think my daughter, Zoe, is Jesus. For a couple of reasons. But before I talk more about her, let's talk about me. You know, since I'm not Jesus and I like talking about myself.

I hate failing. Really hate it, even when it's partly out of my control. I mentioned "My Jesus Project" earlier: the year when I tried to live like Jesus a month at a time. In the month where I focused on "Jesus the Ascetic," I was fasting from solid foods, giving away half of my possessions, practicing a new spiritual discipline each week and reading through the Gospel of Matthew with an ascetic perspective.

A couple of days later, my doctor and dietician pulled me off of my fast because my seizure symptoms had re-emerged (Jesus didn't have epilepsy...cheater). I felt like I had failed, and it took me a day or two to muster the courage to even write about it. Yes, part of the practice was about listening to my body. Yes, another part was to learn to distinguish between my wants and needs. But I had pride at stake, as evidenced by the bruising of said pride when I had to change my diet.

So in a way, the pride at the root of my practice actually was the bigger shortfall. I still ate vegan all month and abstained from alcohol and refined sugar. But I had set a goal and made a public statement about it, and I didn't want to admit I couldn't do it.

Further, my mentor for the month, Reba Riley, called me out, not so much for the shift in diet (well, a little bit), but mostly because of my motivations behind the project. I was struggling, not just with the perceived failure and resulting embarrassment, but also with the fact that I was busting my ass in this practice, far more so than I've ever done for a previous book, and despite grandiose expectations (always the seeds of premeditated resentment), the traffic and overall public response had been pretty lukewarm.

"Why are you doing this?" she asked.

"It seems to me," I said, "that we talk a lot about following Jesus, but most of us don't put a lot of serious energy into figuring out what that really means, day to day, myself included. So I'm taking a year to try and figure it out. And I'm trying to do it in a way that invites other folks to figure it out along with me."

"And you're writing about it."

"Yeah," I said.

"Let me put it this way," she said, "if no one else was watching, if you were doing this only for yourself, would you still do it?" I was silent, partly because I knew the answer.

"I mean, I'd do some of it, but I would spend this much time out of *every day,* and I probably wouldn't give up quite as much."

"Maybe you need to reassess your motivation," she said. "Maybe you're not struggling because people don't seem to care as much as you'd like; maybe it's because your motivations aren't as pure as they should be."

Busted.

Then there's Zoe, our daughter. We've always known she's a mystic. At age three, she announced to us, unsolicited, that she had seen God. I'm not so much for blinding flashes of light and visions, but who can argue with a three-year-old who's seen God?

"Tell me about God."

"She has a big, beautiful face," she smiled, stretching her arms out to her sides.

But there's more than that. I fail and I get frustrated, lose confidence, look for external justifications for my failure and think about giving up. She fails and she just keeps going, over and over again. I've never seen her quit something because it's hard, or even get flustered.

And frankly, it amazes me.

Then there's her generosity. After Halloween, she divides up all of her candy and gives away all of the stuff. I get all of the peanut butter cups. Who knows what else everybody else gets? I mean, I got mine, right? Beyond that, things just pass through her, and yet she always has enough. More than that, she never seems to worry about it.

When her friend, Ben, was having a birthday, she filled a gift bag with all of her toys she thought he'd like. Then before she left for school, I found her in her room emptying her piggy bank. Finally we agreed there might be more noble beneficiaries of her well-earned money.

This week, she figured out who. She brought a box to me from school and set it on my desk. "Do you have any money for me?" she asked. "It's for the kids who are hurting." She's never asked me for money except when she wants to give it to someone else.

"Which kids?" I asked.

"I don't know," she said, looking through the coin slot, "but they need help. Does it matter?"

When you're right, you're right. I pulled all the change out of my pocket, told her to grab whatever coins were on my nightstand, and then gave her one of the dollar coins I had. "Thanks Daddy," she kissed me and ran off to hit up her mom.

Next morning, she was so excited to take the box back to school, she could hardly stand it. So we dumped the contents out to count it. "Umm, Zoe," I puzzled, "you have more than fifty bucks in here."

"Awesome!" she jumped up and down. "That'll help a lot of kids."

"How'd you do that in one day though?"

"I put my money in there," she smiled.

"How much of it?"

"All of it, dad," she looked at me quizzically, "Forty-five dollars. The kids need it."

"Are you sure?"

"Of course," she hugged me. "I'll get more." And with that, she ran off to school, so excited to give away fifteen weeks of her allowance. I couldn't help but think about the widow who gave all she had to the temple.

In that story I was the rich guy, feeling good about handing over pocket change.

Suffice it to say I have a long way to go to figure out this "following Jesus" thing. Sometimes I look to scripture, read books, seek wisdom from my mentors, undergo monthly spiritual practices and try like hell to be more like this guy who supposedly walked the earth two-thousand years ago.

But maybe I just need to start following Zoe around a little more often.

* * *

I started this book by confessing I'm an asshole. And unfortunately even if you finish the last handful of pages, you still will be too. So what's the point, right? Part of it is getting in touch with that reality and hopefully coming to accept it, or maybe even confront it head-on. And I don't think doing so will become an excuse for doing crappy stuff. Hopefully, it'll be an important step toward the kind of honesty and humility Jesus had.

Yes, there's that one text where he says for us to be perfect so maybe we should be without flaw. But maybe he's really telling us we always have unfinished business to work on and don't spend too much time on our yoga poses so we can pat ourselves on the back until we're "capital-P-perfect." Maybe his point was we never will be. Maybe it was less an impossible challenge to make us feel bad, and more to keep us a little challenged, restless.

Yes, we are under construction, but we are worth loving. So let's get real, be willing to be knocked down a few pegs as needed, and keep going. No excuses. No self-deception. No more self-righteousness about how calling ourselves "Christians" makes us better than anyone else. Make a commitment to maintaining the good name Jesus had as a peacemaker, a political visionary of third-way engagement, and a lover of the whole of humanity without boundary or exception.

Yes, it's pretty clear we have a hell of a long way to go.

And it's easy to blame "Church" as a whole for our problems. But that's a dangerously broad brush when talking about a variety of institutions all over the world over thousands of years. Yes, organized religion has done some good in the world, and it's dished out its share of bad stuff. But when we throw Christianity or religion under the bus, we're talking about amoral institutional systems. They're just tools created by human beings to help people know God and live better. Physical spaces for people worshipping, studying, serving and socializing together, their standard practices, are not the issue. "The church" is the people, and if we're assholes, then our best first step is acknowledging that and not judging the assholes around us. Let's be the asshole church together with a commitment to ourselves and each other at least work on it.

The institution, the organization, the system is never going to be perfect. Kind of like the people in them. But punishing a chair by breaking it over your head doesn't really make your pain the chair's fault, does it?

But of course, the church problem is more complicated than that.

Part of it is that some of us are trying to maintain a system that our culture has evolved beyond. That doesn't mean we've outgrown the need for it, but increasingly our society is changing, doing extremely divergent things, and putting lots of time, money and energy into keeping those things going. Why would we meet in a church when we can meet online, in a pub, over a meal, or for coffee or even at a bar?

But we also can't make the same mistake of the Protestant Reformation and just burn it all down, walk away, and start over.

About 127 years ago when I was in college, I was required to learn the history and musical theory behind jazz and blues. I had listened to some jazz, and my dad played blues records some when I was a kid. But like lots of young people, I didn't see the point. I was a rock god, after all! Well, maybe more of a demigod, at least in my own little corner of the north Texas music scene. But it was what I loved, what I knew, and what I wanted to keep doing. Why waste my time learning about some music nerds that died a long time ago, especially when they liked to squawk their horns like dying geese?

The deeper I got into it, though, the more I learned about the story and history behind the music. I started to understand these were the only truly original musical styles to American culture, at least before rap came along. I learned how the blues emerged from the spirituals and folk songs sung by slaves in the southern plantations, and how that sometimes was the only way stories were told for many who never had the opportunity to learn to read. I read about how the oral tradition, and how the oral music tradition of African-Americans in particular, was used sometimes to communicate subversive messages in code among slaves, and how it afforded them at least something that was entirely theirs and helped them express themselves.

From there, jazz emerged as more club-oriented dance music. The word "jazz" actually came from the slang term, "jass," which I'll just say was meant to get female audiences "excited." And while jazz grew and mutated into various other *avant garde* iterations, blues also combined with country and western to give birth to "rock and roll," also named for what those musicians wanted to happen after what "jass" had achieved.

And each subset of musical style had subtler subsets, and each one had its own rules and conventions. Some were more strictly adhered to, while others could be bent and even broken, once you knew what rules you were violating. And what I started to realize was that this chord structure in the song I wrote for my band to play in the clubs in Deep Ellum west of downtown Dallas had its roots in the slave residences and tenement farms of the pre-antebellum south. Even the raunchy lyrics we used to get crowds going–and of course, to get girls–was a decades-old American tradition with the same agenda, but with horns and a bandleader instead of distorted Fender Strats and a frontman in leather pants.

And we thought we were so original.

But there was something both humbling and comforting in knowing my own musical cultural history. It helped me feel like I was part of a much, much longer and richer story than something that had just existed since a handful of bands cranked out some loud and controversial albums on vinyl back in the 70s. It helped me understand my own music on new levels, and it seduced me into a still-ongoing love affair with other styles of music I had previously written off as old and irrelevant.

Most important, at least for me though, was that it helped teach me the rules of music. Now to a rock god(let) like myself, rules were a joke, something to be scoffed at and stomped on with impunity. But how exactly do you do that if you don't even know what rules you're violating or rejecting? Knowing the rules of different styles helped me make better music, not because it made me more like someone else, but because I now understood how to create something I heard in my head for a whole band. It gave me a sort of musical "alphabet" and grammar to help talk with other musicians. And it helped make sense of what I'd been trying to communicate to audiences.

It also gave my music more purpose, and helped define when, how and why I decided to break the rules I was taught. If I wanted to tell a story or evoke a feeling or image, I had so many more tools at my disposal to help me do that. I wasn't just feeling around blindly on my own, hoping my instinct would get me where I wanted to go. It also did something I never would have expected. Knowing the rules didn't hem me in and confine me. It actually helped me add to my playing, my composition and even my enjoyment of music. No one stood over me slapping my wrists if I didn't follow a rule, but now what I did in music seemed to *matter more*. And now I could share and connect with more people in deeper, more interesting ways, which was at least as important as the music itself to me.

It's easy to say "religion is bad and culturally irrelevant" and find plenty of dum-dums to nod in agreement. But that doesn't make it correct, well-informed or of substance, though it might win social points on Facebook or provide an excuse for laziness. Most people want a little bit more out of life than that.

So know where you came from as a creation of both flesh and spirit. Know your ancestry, all of the ways people have interpreted scripture throughout the centuries, ways people worship and why, the symbolism and imagery used in sacred settings and what they mean to different people and groups.

Know the so-called rules that different faiths and denominations adhere to and why some reject particular ones and develop their own. If nothing else, it helps connect you to something that runs so much deeper and broader than just you and your personal experiences. It imbues the acts, prayers, images and texts with richer, more nuanced meaning. It helps make acts of worship more grounding, meaningful, shared, humbling and worthwhile. You do everything with more intention, mindfulness and presence, all of which are values Jesus encouraged us to embrace, irrespective of our cultural background or religious identity. They're the stuff of life, really.

And then if you decide to bend or break a rule or create something new, know why you're doing it. Or if you walk away completely, understand what you're walking away from and what you can take with you. If you decide to reimagine it all in new ways, at least know the stories, lives and meaning behind the things you're changing. In a word, if you're just walking away from something because it's easier, because other people approve or because you fear whatever you don't understand, then the biggest asshole may be in the mirror.

If we use religious communities, systems or practices at all, we should use them to make ourselves, others and the world a better place. Sure, there are other ways to do it, and just because we pick one particular path or the other doesn't inherently make us better than anyone else. But at least we have a chance to find deeper meaning in life, whatever that looks like. Otherwise we're just zombies, whether we're in church or not. We were created for something a hell of a lot better than that.

So let's go figure out what we were made for. Maybe we can even try to figure it out together. I'm willing at least to give it a shot.

ENDNOTES

1 http://www.churchleaders.com/pastors/pastor-articles/139575-7-startling-facts-an-up-close-look-at-church-attendance-in-america.html/5

2 Stephen C. Carlson. The Synoptic Problem Home Page: http://www.mindspring.com/~scarlson/synopt/index.html

3 Jerry L. Walls, "Purgatory for Everyone,"

4 Justo Gonzalez, The Story of Christianity, San Francisco: HarperSanFrancisco (1984): 247.

5 David Harris Sacks, "Imagination in History," Shakespeare Studies 31 (2003)

6 David Harris Sacks "Imagination and History."

7 John Dillenberger, ed., Martin Luther: Selections from His Writings 1st ed., Garden City, NY: Doubleday, (1961): 11.

8 John Dillenberger (1961): 5.

9 Jerry L. Walls, "Purgatory for Everyone," First Things: A Monthly Journal of Religion and Public Life, April 2002.

10 Fredrick Buechner Wishful Thinking: A Seeker's ABC New York: HarperCollins Publishers (1993): 91

GLOSSARY OF CHRISTIANESE

Christians tend to use lots of words and phrases that make no sense to anyone else. Frankly, a lot of Christians don't seem to know what some of them mean, even if they use them. And sometimes they mean different things to different people.

So here are several terms I've collected that some people may need explained.

Advent - Technically means "coming," a time of waiting and preparation for observing Christ's promised birth. Starts on the fourth Sunday before Christmas, and contrary to popular belief, baby Jesus did not come so we could have big retail discounts.

Agape - Although it's spelled like the word "agape" in English, which means "hanging open," this one comes from Greek and is pronounced "uh-GAH-pay." It refers to a sort of universal, unconditional love, like the kind God has for humanity, and that we should learn from. Suffice it to say we generally suck at it, but it's a noble goal.

Altar - Not exclusive to Christianity, but near-universal in worship spaces. A place where sacrifices to God are placed, and often where Christians still place their weekly donations (offerings). Also a place used to place other special items on, like the "communion elements," candles and special things like crosses and big, floppy Bibles.

Anoint - Special oil usually dribbled on someone's head or forehead to invite healing, signify purification or bestow a blessing. Also sometimes used to signify approval for a special role of authority within the church. Also a great way to combat head lice, but makes your hair look a bit unclean.

Apocrypha - This means "hidden," but is often used to refer to books not included in the Bible Protestants (i.e. non-Catholics) accept and refer to today. Some people question their authenticity or feel like they don't align with the teachings of the rest of the biblical texts, while others feel they're just as valid and hold necessary wisdom. For some, the Bible is already so long and dense, it's like when your aunt gives you that un-edited "Left Behind" boxed set for Christmas. Seriously, are you ever gonna read all that?

Apostate - A word used for someone who is believed to have turned their backs on some belief or value held as important to the church. It's another word for "outcast" (outcast with a "C," not a K. Cause we all know that Andre 3000 is awesome sauce).

Atone/Atonement - To make amends or make right for some kind of screw-up. Usually used in conjunction with being "cleansed from sin." It's often used to convict of guilt and the need to express remorse and repentance in order to accept Jesus' "substitution" through his sacrificial death as "payment" for our sin. I don't know about you, but I get my sins at Costco in bulk for $9.95 a gross. I know I'm never gonna use them all but it's such a good deal, it's like they're paying me!

Baptism - How to show you're in the club. Depending where you get yours done, it involves a pastor or church leader either getting you a little wet or totally submerged. Some sprinkle holy water on babies, others wait until you ask for it yourself, and then you'll find out whether you'll be dunked forward 3 times or just once backwards. Some believe baptism is the only way to get all the benefits of Christian membership, but for others it's more of a symbol of lifelong commitment to Jesus. Back in ancient times, people were baptized naked which probably went out about the time people started having potluck dinners afterward.

Benediction - Usually an offering of affirmation, hope or blessing offered by the minister at the end of a worship service before people leave. Literally, means "good word" from the Latin words *bene* and *dictum*. Yes, I know what that last word sounds like. Just don't be the smartass who shares that at coffee hour.

Bible Belt - There's no official boundary line, but generally agreed to be a geographical swatch across the United States including Arkansas, Mississippi, Alabama, Tennessee, Kentucky, Georgia, and North and South Carolina where conservative Christianity has its largest presence. Dallas is sometimes considered the sparkly rhinestone on the buckle. If you're from this area, you're a default Christian. And definitely not the progressive kind.

Blended Worship - A worship service that contains both older and newer elements. "Traditional worship" involves songs that are hundreds of years old; "Contemporary worship" songs are only about 10-20 years old. Combined, it's a solid attempt to make everyone happy, which isn't really churches' job, but hey, it keeps the peace and brings those Benjamins coming in, yo.

Bless/Blessing/Blessed - As a verb, to offer favor or help. As a noun, either a prayer of thanks, or presumptuous suggestion of God's supposed favor ("#Blessed"). Unfortunately, the word has been coopted to suggest those who use it are extra special because God evidently loves to "bless" us while kids starve to death in Africa. Want to be a myopic, self-serving jerk? Well, blessings on you!

Body of Christ - Either in reference to the bread in the ritual of communion (as in the "body broken for you"), or to those committed to following Jesus. Some are more Christlike, while others of us are more like that "clone of a clone of a clone of a person" in the movie *Multiplicity* that ends up wearing underwear on his head and licking slices of pizza. Not so good.

Born Again - Jesus told Nicodemus the Pharisee he had to be "born again," as in leave behind his old way of thinking and living and be reborn of the spirit. It's been used to describe dramatic conversion experiences, and often to draw a distinction between the kind of Christian who has gone through such a transformation, and everyone else who still needs to if they want to go to heaven. It's another unfortunate redefinition. I suggest using that line from *The Princess Bride*, "You keep using that word. I do not think it means what you think it means."

Brother/Sister in Christ - Other believers trying to be like Jesus. Sometimes evoked to convict members of the Christian country club of something they're doing or thinking about doing. Because everyone feels guiltier about doing wrong when you're in a family.

C-and-E ("a C-and-E Christian?) - An insider term for folks who come to church only twice a year–Christmas and Easter. Used to generalize about those who come only because family or moral obligation pressures them to, but not because they travel for work or are often away from home on Sundays. Usually a favorite of overworked staffers and sort of a more polite way to complain about low attendance.

Cannon - The set of texts approved by the Council of Nicea as "the official Bible." Any other texts are "extra-cannonical," even heretical, which gives the inerrancy argument its firepower and also helps to define the phrase "weaponizing the Bible."

Chancel - Similar to "narthex," an ancient word used to make the area toward the front of the church sound special. And since it's usually where the altar is located, the choir sings and where the preacher speaks, it kind of is. Incidentally, the "regular folk" sit in the "nave" and it's all reminiscent of the time when pompous priests banned people from even entering certain areas of the church. I'm not sure what was so special that happened up there, but I'm pretty sure it involved beer pong. Good news is we don't have any self-righteous religious leaders anymore. So....yeah.

Christ - Translates directly as "messiah" or "anointed one" which doesn't clear things up at all for most people. Refers to the one promised by ancient prophets to be specially sent by God to bring salvation, either to keep your goodies out of hell for all eternity, or to release us from the world's bondage. Either way, it is not, according to Scripture, Jesus' last name. And no, his middle initial isn't "H" either.

Communion - A symbolic meal instituted by Jesus the night before he was arrested by the Roman authorities. It was during the Jewish holiday of Passover, so he used what was nearby—bread and wine—using the two "elements" as symbols representing his Jesus' willingness to hand himself and surrender it all in the name of selfless, sacrificial love. Christians use it to remember Jesus' death weekly, monthly, or a few times a year, differing widely on what it really means. Some think it's pointing to his need to die and have his blood shed to make up for human sin, while others think it's more of a rallying cry for all of us to live out radically "sacrificial love" every day. Or you can think of it as a little, tiny mini-brunch to hold you over: "Jeez-its" if you will.

Contemporary Worship - Usually a worship service including electric guitars, drums or both, and more "modern" music, though most songs may be from the seventies and eighties. Often used to attract younger people to church, but tending to appeal mostly to baby boomers. Younger folks know it's definitely not contemporary.

Deacon - Sort of "layperson officers" in the church. They serve communion, help collect offering, serve as ushers or greeters, and other stuff that needs doing. It's usually something asked of people who are active in the church and are on board with the vision and mission. If you go up to them and call them "Deacon Blue" like Steely Dan said to in that song, you'll usually get nothing but blank stares.

Denomination - An affiliated group of churches that embrace a shared idea about "true" church doctrine and religious rules and have a common system of governance. Some, like the Christian Church (Disciples of Christ), have little to no hierarchy or carved-in-stone tenets all adherents have to claim. Others, like Episcopalians, have more top-down governance and a pretty consistent set of doctrines from church to church. Fun fact: there are more than 12,000 denominations within Christianity now, which means if all but one are wrong, you're mathematically screwed.

Devotions/Devotional - A regular practice of prayer or reflection. Usually a short piece of writing with scripture to read and ponder, either thematic or topical to guide prayer. As a way to pursue regular spiritual practice and connect with God. Kinda like yoga, but without all the pain and need for stretchy athletic wear. Though athletic devotions are probably a thing now too.

Doxology - A liturgical church word meaning short prayer of praise to God, usually sung. Obviously, more old-school and traditional, and used by people who don't mind using words that make no sense to anyone else.

Elder - Sounds like an insult, but actually a term of honor for those appointed to seve the church behind closed doors and make the decisions with the staff. Just to confuse people, you don't have to be old to be an elder, but you do have to demonstrate wisdom and a heart for service. Also not a sort of "lifetime achievement award" to say thanks to someone before they kick the bucket.

Emerging/Emergent - A network of communities that, somewhat ironically, tend to push back or reject categorization. For some it means "liberal church," and for others, "contemporary," i.e. "relevant." Asking an emergent Christian if they're emergent is kind of like asking a hipster if they're a hipster. Only politicians have such wordy non-answers to a question. Interestingly, confusion is definitely a bit of what emergent is about.

End-times - Used more by evangelicals than other types of Christians, it's happy, good news for the "saved," bad for everyone else. Often used as a warning for non-believers to get their holy underwear on before it's too late. People are obsessed with the apocalypse and movies and book series make millions off it every year. It's sort of some Christians' hobby to discuss how it's all gonna go down.

Epiphany - A Christian holiday (and beginning of the liturgical season of Epiphany) also known as "Three Kings Day." It commemorates the day when God was revealed to the three kings (who eventually made a trek to Bethlehem) in the form of Jesus' birth. Were there really three kings? Hmm. Not sure. Is it a real holiday? Probably not. Which is why no one knows about it.

Evangelism - Literally, to "share the good news." And of course, what that "good news" means varies a lot depending which Christian you ask. For some it's about telling others that Jesus died for their sins, while for others it's about sharing that Jesus was God. For some, it means telling others "Jesus saves" and preaching to as many people as will listen. "Servant evangelism" is about living one's witness without necessarily using words or explaining one's beliefs. Great for growing a church.

Excommunicate - To be kicked out of a church or denomination for bad behavior. In Catholicism it is often due to divorce or some sinful act deemed unforgivable. But it's also an efficient way to weed out troublemakers who question authority, want to change stuff, or pee in the baptistry.

Fire Insurance - A derogatory term for an understanding of Christian salvation as only or primarily about keeping people from going to hell. And the lucky bastards who have it can also claim flood insurance since God promised that big flood won't happen again.

Gospel - "Good news," literally, but meaning varies widely. For some, the Good News is all about Jesus' death and salvation of sin. For others, it's as simple as "God Loves you." In liberation theology, a release from bondage and repression, including bondage of sin. Some brands of Christianity have turned it into bad news by focusing too much on sin and not enough on grace. But that doesn't change the fact that it's a big term with a good story at the center. Though I wish it did, I don't think the Mavericks beating the Spurs counts as this kind of good news. A guy can dream though.

Grace - Unmerited freedom from a rule, expectation or obligation. A confusing concept, even for Christians, and very difficult not to continually forget. It means forgiving without limit and loving unconditionally, which is tricky. Usually we want a thank-you card, an email or even a text, for crying out loud. Is a text too much to ask??? Oh yeah, grace...

Hedge of Protection - Metaphysical shrubbery evoked as spiritual barrier against the forces of evil, similar to a Holy Spirit force field. Adapted from Job 1:8, very spiritual Christians are well acquainted with the magical properties of the H.O.P. Though a bush may not seem to offer much protection, demons and sinful temptations alike cower before it. Must be one stinky hedge.

Heretic - Often, someone who's really gotten on the wrong side of a self-important Christian, and gets applied in many cases it doesn't really apply. Often used as an accusation against those challenging a tradition, belief or doctrine, e.g. Martin Luther, Galileo, Copernicus, and may eventually mean "badass catalyst who finally brought about real change."

Holy Spirit - Widely regarded as the coolest member of the Holy Trinity. As opposed to "Father God" or "Almighty God," and the Son, Jesus, the Holy Spirit (aka Holy Ghost, or to the ancient Celts, "the wild goose") is more mystical and represented in scripture as many things—a dove, wind, fire, etc. Some consider it a more feminine expression of God while others think of it as "God within," whereas Father is "God beyond" and Son is "God among." Which may make the Holy Spirit the best one to pray to about excess gassiness.

Lent - The 40 days leading up to Easter when Christians consider their mortality and reflect on Jesus' sacrifice, often involving giving something up, like meat, television, or meat television if you're into that. The word comes from the word "lengthen," because days start getting longer after Ash Wednesday (aka ash-smudging-on-your-forehead day, or "see-how-many-weird-looks-you-can-get-on-the-bus day").

Life Verse - A particularly obnoxious invention intended to help people take a verse or couple of verses completely out of context and apply it to their own life like a talisman to ward off evil or bring them good luck. It's usually considered to be formative in their Christian identity and daily journey. Basically, it's their favorite verse, for whatever reason.

Liturgy/Liturgical - There are a couple of meanings to this. One refers to an order of worship shared by an entire denomination. It can also refer to the Liturgical calendar, which lays out the entire year in seasons, like Lent, Pentecost, Advent and the like. It also breaks up the Bible thematically so a preacher, if they follow the liturgical calendar, can preach through most of the bible over three years. I guess the parts they leave out are less important, like how to cook salmon or lace up those weird sandals they used to wear.

Miracle - An event that can't be explained by reason but requires faith and is attributed to an act of God. Sometimes people, places or things are considered a "miracle," though the Catholic Church has stricter rules about this, which of course they do.

Missional - A church devoted to missions and not a building, i.e. "radical," "social-justice-seeking," i.e. "turned inside-out." Describes a difference of focus, instead of bringing people in, sending people out into the community. Also a cute catchphrase used to sound trendy while not really changing much of substance.

Narthex - The lobby or gathering area just outside the worship space, derived from Greek and originally the area where people making good for their sins had to stay until they were pure enough to enter into the sacred worship space. So yeah, sorry folks, everyone should probably be worshiping in the Narthex from now on.

Offering - A churchgoer's weekly contribution to the church. Sometimes called "tithe," meant both as spiritual discipline of sacrifice and as a way to keep the church and associated ministries going. Offering usually follows the sermon, unless the preaching isn't good enough to empty those pockets, in which case, it precedes it.

Pastor - Leader of the church, head dude or lady, administrator (usually), preacher (often) and so-called "shepherd of the flock." Which means when people get out of line, they get to whack them with a big stick...right? Damn. Actually, it's basically the chief bag-holder and the one who gets blamed when things go south. Good thing that never, ever happens.

Pentecost/Pentecostal - From Greek, meaning "fiftieth day" for the fiftieth day after the "Shavuot" or Feast of Weeks in the Jewish Passover. Christians have repurposed "the day of Pentecost" to remind of the Holy Spirit coming to the disciples and inspiring them to spread the Gospel. Pentecostal is a denomination known for yelling preachers, and people talking in tongues and falling on the floor and wiggling from inspiration of the Holy Spirit, which for some reason other folks reportedly find "weird."

Popcorn Prayer - A cute name for inviting anyone in a given group to pray freely, kinda like Mad Libs, but more spontaneous. Often an opportunity to learn more than you'd like to about the people you're worshiping with, which is why they don't let me say anything during popcorn prayers anymore.

Praise - Giving thanks or worshiping God and expressing gratitude, usually in word or in song. Often a reminder to give credit to God for the good in our lives, intended to keep people humble and less asshole-y.

Praise Band/Team - A group of 3 or 14 people that leads the more "contemporary" worship music part of the church service. Often incorporating such modern instruments as guitars, drums and electronic keyboards, they have unusually high energy and are meant to be more inspiring than regular congregants, It's like a rock concert but without the....well without the rock and the concert. So I guess it's really not like that.

Prayer Warrior - A person very skilled in and often designated as the praying person in a congregation. May take requests and/or "intercede" on behalf of others, particularly the pastor and church leaders. Often an unofficial designation in more evangelical communities they may be seen as a sort of "hedge of protection" against evil spirits for the church. And it's super awesome when you get them to say, "I ain't afraid of no ghosts."

Prophet/Prophetic - Either a sort of Christian fortune teller, or simply someone who sees reality as it truly is and speaks their insights to help and/or influence people. Prophets take many forms beyond "you all suck and you're gonna burn in hell" kind. Martin Luther King was a prophet, as was Gandhi. You don't have to be a Christian to be prophetic, neither do you have to be into "the prophetic" to be Christian, though "prophetic Christians" tend to disagree. Normal people tend to dislike that prophets aren't like them, but if they were, they probably wouldn't be very good prophets.

Protestant - As opposed to Catholics, Christians from the movement inspired by Martin Luther who broke away from the hierarchy and legalism of the Catholic church to establish direct access to God without ordained mediators or interpreters, though Christians keep trying to add intermediaries back in, which kinda defeats the whole point," but that's a different topic.

Psalm - A prayer in the form of a song, as found in the book of Psalms in the Bible. Many are believed to have been written by King David, who reportedly praised God by stripping down and dancing around the city in his birthday suit. And this, kids, is called scriptural support for naked worship.

Purpling - Uncommon, but something youth leaders may have said to remind people at overnight co-ed events not to make babies. As far as anyone can tell, the idea is that boys are blue, girls are pink, so no making purple." Get it? Yeah it's cheesy and dumb, but it's probably better than saying "Okay kids, have fun, but no putting penises in vaginas, okay?" And then follows the chorus of parental heart attacks.

Rapture - Related to "end times," the point in history as some Christians believe, when the faithful are evacuated by God up to heaven while everyone else is left behind to suck it and/or hold post-rapture parties before all the scary shit goes down.

Redeemed/Redemption - Related to salvation, someone reconciled to or made right with God, or the act of being reconciled or made right. Usually related to being "born again" (or being baptized), though for most, it's about being pure, clean of sin. For some, the word conjures images of grocery coupons or vouchers, though they probably aren't very spiritual.

Repent - To formally or personally reject sin in favor of a more virtuous life (or salvation, see below). "Light" version involves asking God for forgiveness but not really changing much, whereas more sincere variety is evidenced by a changed life.

Salvation - The state of being saved from going to hell. Or being healed of something, be it a broken heart, recovering from addiction or learning to love more fully. Similar to Sanctify, there's considerable debate about salvation is achieved, but most agree it isn't by drinking laced Kool-Aid, freezing your severed head, or winning a pie-eating contest. Mmmmmm, pie.

Sanctify - To make something sacred, i.e. set apart as particularly holy, i.e. "holy" mean? It's ain't the kind in my underwear, I can tell you that. Geez, you ask a lot of questions!

Sanctuary - Originally "sacred place," and a place of safety, now refers to the large room for weekly services where members of a church gather, sort of like the living room of a house. Christian sanctuaries usually contain a cross, and are often decorated (or undecorated) to reflect the values of members and leadership. Some view it as sacred, others simply as different from "the world" and other churches.

Scripture - The Bible, "Holy Bible," "Holy Word (of God)," "God's (Holy) Word," "Holy scripture," "Holy writ," "The Word," etc. Most people say it's just what is in "the Bible," thought if you read the rest of this book, you know even that is up for debate. And if you didn't, march yourself straight to the cashier and put some money down, mister! I ain't doin' this for my health!

Sin - Anything that separates humanity from God. Known as "*hamartia*" in Greek, literally "missing the mark," usually it references impure thought or action. If someone's using the term, odds are good it has something to do with other people's naughty bits.

Spiritual Birthday - The day you became a Christian (or in some churches, got baptized). Commie liberal Christians don't observe this, likely because the zombies that made us this way also erased our memory. What was I saying?

Sword Drill - Derived from Eph. 6:17 "the sword of the Spirit, which is the word of God," refers to an informal test most often performed by youth pastors in the 80s and 90s to help students learn to study and memorize the Bible. Or in my case, to help a student learn to duck a Bible being chucked at them. Let's hear it for biblically-inspired violence!

Testimony - (also see Witness below) Your personal story of accepting the good news and/or becoming a Christian. Also refers to an inspiring sales pitch used by someone who attends a "Bible-believing" church. And sometimes means, "I'm an asshole who believes in coercing people to believe what I believe for the sake of their soul."

Tract - A little pamphlet laying out the basic principles of Christian faith and why someone should believe (often used with witnessing, see below). Apparently, some Christians leave a tract instead of a tip at a restaurant, which makes you wonder if that doesn't make the good news seem a bit like "cheap grace."

Traveling Mercies - A superficial way to say you're praying someone has a safe trip, especially if the person traveling is someone you want to think you're very spiritual (see "Bless/Blessing/Blessed"). It's basically useless insurance, but unlike most insurance, actually costs you nothing. So really, nothing like insurance at all.

Witness - The act of sharing your testimony, i.e. publicly talking about how you became a Christian. Also usually involves sharing principles of the Christian faith and inviting people to your church (and sometimes scaring them into it). Most of the time you won't hear non-evangelicals talking about witnessing. That is, unless they were witnessed *to*. Then it's more like passing on the legacy of fraternal hazing.

The Word - Written, this refers to text in the Bible. Spoken, this usually refers to a sermon. Basically it means words inspired by God...so basically just the Bible. And, of course, this book.

WWJD - Acronym for "What Would Jesus Do?" Though this is a good question to be reminded of on a regular basis, it became more of a marketing cliché emblazoned on swag to make it more "Christian." Kind of like "FUBU" but with more Jesus sprinkled on top. What would Jesus do? Probably resist pandering to a consumerist agenda with Jesus junk. But that's just a guess.